Why You No Scream?! Viva?!

My Big Mexican Adventure that taught me how to Live, Love, and Laugh Again

Brooke Martellaro

HUGO HOUSE PUBLISHERS, LTD.

ISBN: 978-1-936449-54-5

Library of Congress Control Number: 2013943658

Limits of Liability and Disclaimer of Warranty

The author and publisher shall not be liable for your misuse of this material. This book is strictly for informational and educational purposes.

Warning—Disclaimer

The purpose of this book is to educate and entertain. The author and/or publisher do not guarantee that anyone following these techniques, suggestions, tips, ideas, or strategies will become successful. The author and/or publisher shall have neither liability nor responsibility to anyone with respect to any loss or damage caused, or alleged to be caused, directly or indirectly by the information contained in this book.

Cover Design and Interior Layout: www.taylorbydesign.com

Illustrator: Kaitlyn Whyte

Contents

PART ONE: GRIEVING AND OPENING TO SERENDIPITY – DISCOVERING PLAYA

Introduction

*W**HY** **Y**OU **N**O **S**CREAM **V**IVA?! **L**EARNING TO **L**IVE, **L**OVE, AND **L**AUGH*
Again is a tale of life interrupted… or so it seemed at the time.
There we were, Brooke and I, progressing along with our lives as planned,
fulfilling the roles that caused our paths to cross. I was pulled into the
story by a number of magnetic forces, not the least of which was the
vulnerability and need of the main character herself.

Before this tale began, I did not know Brooke well. Our contact was
primarily professional. On the days that I saw her, she was a genuine
pleasure to work for, but she was frequently absent—conscientious in
her role as the most dedicated workaholic that I have ever met. I often
found myself wondering if she had many friends outside of work and
Marc. She was always either working or traveling. Always.

Little did I know that I would end up stepping into the role of companion in a big way. With her sudden, startling break-up, I somehow
landed myself the privilege of her friendship and trust… and I began
to uncover one of my favorite people.

You see, Brooke has a way of winning one's heart, disarming one.
She is a combination of your favorite, slightly naive high school pal,
and the hot redhead that all of the guys are too shy to talk to. Somehow
she still retains that sense of innocence combined with a spirit of play,
making you think that whatever caper you're in the middle of is the most
exciting thing that you've ever done. She's refreshing in a way that few
people are—able to offer advice backed up with a frank, no-nonsense
do-the-right-thing attitude. She's got a brain the size of Texas, and yet
she's willing to drop everything and act as an accomplice to the most
ridiculous of antics. She's the kind of person you want on your team.

WHY YOU NO SCREAM VIVA?!

But I get ahead of the tale. Herein lies the series of events that helped to build a change in this spectacular individual.

I invite readers to immerse themselves in this story of lost love and found self. Many of these events and the lessons therein apply to all of us women. If you've been through it, you'll relate.

Do read on and join our journey! Seize the day!

Kim Magee
May, 2013

FOREWORD

AS MY GREAT FRIEND KIM SAID IN THE INTRODUCTION, I WAS A workaholic at the beginning of this tale, but due to the events depicted in this true-to-life book, I have moved beyond "holic" to "holistic"—a balanced life of creating meaning, growth and joy; whether in work or play and in all relationships and life endeavors. Perhaps it is my foremost purpose in life to find and keep this balance and to help others find their ideal balance at any given time. So, while I am still a finance professional in Colorado, I also lead custom-made, life-enhancing workshops in my beloved Playa del Carmen, Mexico, where most of this book takes place. This magical place served as a catalyst for my regaining the excitement and magic of living fully, authentically and with great joy.

At age thirty-nine, I became devastated by a traumatic break-up with my life partner of eleven years and my world shrunk to the size of my navel—(at which I was spending too much time staring and contemplating.) In the recovery process I learned so much and had so many grand adventures, I just had to write this book.

Why You No Scream Viva?! is a book of my simple stories based on the escapades, adventures and events taking place (mostly) on the Mayan Riviera and the "characters" that peopled them. This book not only reveals my recovery from the harrowing break-up—a retrieval of self that began in Playa del Carmen, Mexico—but also highlights all the risks I decided to take to regain, develop and expand my sense of self and to find my place in this world with more self-awareness and love.

With a little help from those rascally pals serendipity and synchronic-ity and the friendship of one trusted friend, Kim, I was able to become more and more alive, more and more me, instead of shrinking back from life after loss and disappointment. I had to connect with my intuition and common sense, my courage, insight and innate generosity of heart to get out there and make things happen in ways that surprised and challenged me. In short, I had to redefine myself. For me the process required grieving, opening to serendipity, finding my healing place, taking new risks, taking massive, decisive action, getting back in the game, getting grounded and moving on. I had to learn not to flinch from the negative but to embrace, understand and deal with it while learning how to always *choose* the positive way to resolve and rise above it.

While this book is mostly memoir, I call it a book "based on real events" because although about ninety-five percent of the events did occur; a very few were invented to flesh out a thought or feeling that did occur to me. Some of the dialogue was also invented, but the intention behind the words is true and real. I changed most of the names, except for Kim, Cindy, Sarah, River, Meko, Dexter the Dog, Marc, Mark and Mark (yes, there are three with that name). I honor each "character" in my story. I am grateful to them for what I learned because of their presence in my life.

Life is ironic. Sometimes the most tragic events in your life can end up being the biggest blessings of all. Life is also comical. In reflecting back on everything that happened during the "recovery" years, including all the pain, I found humor in almost every little thing that happened. Part of my recovery necessitated embracing my sense of humor, however quirky it may be, and it threads through the book. I want to persuade my readers and workshop participants that it's so important to be able to laugh at yourself and find lightness in your life's journey—even if you have to wait a few years to see the humor and hidden treasure in it all. We really should stop taking ourselves so seriously. Seriously!

I've written this book for women in all stages of relationships with others and with themselves. For all you women out there who don't yet see that your past heartbreaks are really gifts; opportunities for you to grow into the amazing, strong, compassionate women that you are at your cores, I invite your transformation into gratitude and happiness.

Foreword

For those of you still stinging from loss or betrayal, my story may offer perspective and some workable ideas about moving on. Perhaps you are not stuck in the depths of despair but have just given up a little on finding the joy of living, loving, and the magic of connecting with people. I hope my book will encourage you to find delight again.

I also wrote *Why You No Scream Viva?!* to speak to anyone who finds herself at a crossroads in life and is looking for inspiration to charge forward again and create her life anew. Risk-taking can be surprisingly rewarding, I found.

In writing my stories of this time period in my life, I wanted to capture some of the enchantment I found—being, living and working in Playa del Carmen—even if I could not define exactly what it was at the time. That enchantment continues to impact and give meaning to my life. At the same time, the challenges I faced while living in the Riviera Maya, involved considerable pain and loss of innocence without which I would not have learned some of life's most important lessons and messages.

Finally, this book is a love story. A story about falling out of love with a persona I built around a particular man and a particular lifestyle. And a story about falling in love with a new persona built around the spiritual being I truly am. I fell in love: with me, with friends, with other men, with my life and with all the beauty and wonderment of this world.

I wish I could say that I thought up this brilliant strategy on my own and executed it flawlessly. But the fact is, I stumbled into this journey—at least at the beginning. I now genuinely feel I was being guided by my own inner voice to take this journey so that I could come out the other side a stronger, more vibrant woman and then share my experience with the world to help others find their own necessary journey.

The ethereal is part of the Mayan Spell, believe me, but there is a grounded reality that comes along with it. In my journey to Maya, I found both the highest natural high and the most down-to-earth realities ever. Both of these elements make us strong and certain, and don't we all want those things? I hope you will be able to connect to a place within you that is beyond laughter and tears; a vast, wondrous space wherein you find treasures of your heart and soul as yet undiscovered.

I'll leave you with my new, favorite motto: "Be the kind of woman that when your feet hit the floor each morning, the devil says, 'Oh, crap, she's up!'" Anonymous.

Brooke Martellaro
May, 2013

The most beautiful things in the world

cannot be seen or even touched.

They must be felt within the heart.

~ Helen Keller ~

PART ONE

Grieving and Opening to Serendipity – Discovering Playa

༄ ༄ ༄

Challenges are what make life interesting;
Overcoming them is what makes life meaningful.

~ Joshua J. Marine ~

Chapter 1

THE BREAK-UP

"**B**ALNEARIO; THAT'S WHERE WE'RE GOING FOR CHRISTMAS," MY faithful friend Kim declares, as she once again assures me I will survive the break-up.

BAHL-neh-AH-reeh-OH. Where's Balneario? I think. I've traveled all over the world and I've never heard of it. Maybe that's a country in the Indonesian islands, near Bali. Kim loves that part of the world. Yeah, I'll bet that's where we're going. "Cool, I've never been to that country," I respond. "It's not a country, silly. *Balneario* is the word for a Latin American seaside resort. We're going to Playa del Carmen, Mexico."

"Oh, okay. Why didn't you just say so?" I scoff. Having been equally well-traveled around the world, she is obviously expanding my travel horizons and improving my vocabulary at the same time. (Note to self, look up *Balneario* on Wikipedia.)

If I can muster the energy, this will be the latest attempt to run away from what has become my life.

Okay, deep breath, Brooke. You see, I have recently found myself dumped by my boyfriend. What a concept, "dumped." Who invented that term, anyway? Dump is what you do with the garbage. Grrrr. Why can't we say "released" instead? Would changing the word soften the blow?

Anyway, I'm figuring out who I am as a single woman for the first time in twenty years. Marc and I have been in a committed relationship for the past eleven years and prior to that I was in a nine-year relationship

1

with my ex-husband. I know this sounds pathetic, but being "released" from a lifestyle of traveling first-class around the world seems to be way worse than being released from a lifestyle of traveling road-warrior style around the state. I'm just sayin'...

Okay, so I've decided. The word "released" does *not* soften the blow. I think about Marc's new girlfriend who now resides in *my* house. "Dumped" by the curb like a pile of last month's magazines is definitely how it feels. Oh, and did I mention that I'm about to turn forty in a few weeks? Grrrr.

The thought of starting my life over and dating again at age forty is S-C-A-R-Y. I was a very different person at age twenty—a mischievous, adventurous college student with no life experience. Dating was just a party. But, for the last decade or so, I've created my identity as part of a worldly couple on the go, way more than as an individual. At my age, we all have more life experience, more loss, and more baggage. And I wonder, *regarding dating, have the rules changed?*

Not only are all my future dreams with my ex shattered, as I said, so is my jetsetter lifestyle of globetrotting around the world. If this sounds materialistic to you, let me point out some positive intangibles to that lifestyle: freedom to move, to see, and to connect with an immense part of this amazing planet. My world, over the past eleven years, had become huge (literally and figuratively).

On the other hand, money does not buy happiness, or should I say, joy. The last six months of our relationship were not as blissful as the other ten and a half years, despite the luxurious vacations. Even in the best Paris penthouse you can find, if the connection with your lover is gone, the scenery can look rather bleak and the Eiffel tower can look like just a pretty heap of metal.

Kim is ever to the rescue, offering physical space and probably hoping upon hope that I will free up my mental and emotional space. She's offering time out from my rapidly shrinking life and introverted mental state with plans to go to Mexico.

The Break-Up

    If it wasn't for my caring friend, I might stew in this forever. So, I'll do this for her. I talk to myself (as I do a lot these days.) *Okay, Brooke, time to get off this pity party merry-go-round and start living again!*

Chapter 2

THE GREAT ESCAPE

I<small>T'S 7:00 A.M., ON</small> M<small>ONDAY</small>, D<small>ECEMBER</small> 19, <small>JUST SIX DAYS BEFORE</small> Christmas. We are flying on a chartered air-bus down to Playa del Carmen, Mexico. I'm exhausted, having been up drinking adult beverages until 2:00 a.m. at a Christmas party the night before. I try eating a breakfast sandwich from the airport McDonald's, but my body is having no part in that. I lost my appetite two months ago, when "The Tragedy" occurred. The good thing is, I shed twenty pounds in two weeks. No joke. Best diet I've ever been on.

I ask Kim, who has been my constant companion since that shocking day, "Is this what single women in their forties do for fun these days? Stay out half the night drinking and then head off to unknown foreign locations in a large metal tube that could be mistaken for a cattle car?"

She frowns, "Cattle car? Brooke, you are clearly either delirious or still inebriated. Get some sleep." She herself looks physically and emotionally drained, having taken care of me over the past eight weeks and also working like a dog just before the holidays. She turns back to her pile of magazines as if whatever she's looking at is the most interesting thing she's ever read.

Am I whining? I've got to stop that. Take a nap, Brooke.

ೞ ೞ ೞ

5

Several hours later, we arrive at El Dorado Royale, the all-inclusive resort just outside of town we will call home for the next week. Wikipedia said that a *balneario* is: "A Latin American seaside resort offering recreation, sports, entertainment, food, hospitality, retail and cultural events - characterized by being flooded by masses of tourists during the summer seasons." Well, okay, even though it is winter, this is what we're getting.

We walk into the resort on wobbly legs. But, my God, it's love at first sight! The resort is all white marble and tile. The air, while balmy, is fresh and smells sweet. As we climb the stairs to the lobby, I notice the grounds are impeccably landscaped with palm trees, agave plants and aloe vera. The huge lobby is an indoor/outdoor setting with big, red bromeliads strategically placed. They have also decorated with red and white poinsettias everywhere which reminds me that it is Christmastime, even in Mexico.

As we look out from the lobby toward the ocean, there are two spiraling staircases leading down to the heart of the resort. In between the two staircases are more palm trees, cacti and my favorite plant of all, bougainvillea. They have intertwined both white and bright pink bougainvillea. I breathe in the sweetness of the flowers and taste the salty air on my lips. A feeling of comfort and familiarity washes over me. A familiarity of that cherished feeling of freedom I had in my travels with Marc.

Will I ever find a partner as adventurous as Marc again? Or is there a reason why they give you black balloons when you turn forty?

I drift back to the present, taking a deep breath. I am breathing less shallowly here, that's good. What is it about this air? The breeze wafting in and out of the buildings is unencumbered by screens or window frames or even walls—posts and columns hold up the rooftops for the most part. Everywhere I look I see fantastic flora.

I roll my suitcase over to a giant, exotic arrangement of birds-of-paradise mixed in with the most startling flowers and succulents not even a parrot could outdo in colors. I just stand there admiring them, breathing them in, feeling suddenly about five years old because they tower above me and I'm lost in wonder. The flowers seem to whisper, "You are vibrant, vivid and beautifully colorful just as we are."

Before I can shut down that optimistic voice with my own negative view of getting older, I feel a tiny opening in my heart and am surprised by a sudden, if fleeting, feeling that I am ageless. *I'm experiencing chills and a kind of thrill goes through my body then is gone. Interesting... I just vacillated between ages five and thirty-nine in a matter of moments. What a weird out-of-body experience I am having. I want to have that ageless feeling again. Can we choose our age, no matter how many years we've been on this earth?*

Chapter 3

SLEEPING BEAUTIES

A FTER CHECKING INTO THE RESORT AND CHECKING OUT THE grounds, Kim and I both lie down to take a little nap. Ever experience lying down for a nap and suddenly feeling like your body weighs one thousand pounds? Our sighs of relief could have set off an alarm if there was such a thing as a sigh detector.

Yes, we are both physically and emotionally exhausted. Me, from weeping and blubbering twelve out of sixteen waking hours of the day, every day for the last two months. *How is the body able to manufacture that much water? Poor body—no wonder you're so wrung out.* And Kim, I'm guessing, must be exhausted from being my emotional crutch for the last sixty days, while still maintaining some semblance of her own life. Imagine someone calling you every couple of hours every day for two months just to sob about every little thing which reminded that person of their now defunct life. It was actually hard to find anything that *didn't* remind me of Marc. But poor Kim, listening to my pity parties must not have been an easy job, for sure. I'm amazed we actually remained friends until this day.

Note to self: I am going to have to elevate Kim to the status of "Saint Kim."

℀ ℀ ℀

Some six hours later, it's dark outside, not a creature is stirring, and we awaken to discover that we have officially slept away our first day of vacation! Crap! We didn't want to miss out on anything.

Since we are both still feeling a little sleepy, we decide to order room service—*Nachos, por favor*. Room service discreetly knocks and a young Latino man presents us with a little tray and then slips out again.

"What's this?" we both exclaim in unison. Their version of nachos looks nothing like my beloved heaping mound of chips, cheese and all the toppings. We stare down at the plate of twelve chips, beans and a smidge of some type of indistinguishable cheese, look at each other and just laugh! There's no meat, no salsa, no jalapenos, no guacamole, no sour cream. Nope, just some triangles, beans and that teensy bit of cheese. I would not recommend room-service nachos unless you are a minimalist type of eater—which we become this night because we're still too punch-drunk to dress up and go eat someplace to fill our famished bellies.

We watch a little TV and then I crack open my chosen reading for the trip, a book titled *Narcissism*. I've been suspecting that my ex is a narcissist, and I'm determined to understand what makes a narcissist tick. That way, maybe I can understand him better when we get back together, which I'm positive will happen. *He's just having a temporary fling, right?*

We agree to have lights out at 9:00 p.m., for a good night's sleep to get an early start on the next day, since we slept away our first day. For some reason this reminds me of summer camp as a young girl. I remember how we were forever trying to break the "lights out" rule by staying up as late as we could, whispering and giggling. Then the camp counselor would give us the talk about how we had growing bodies and needed lots of sleep to enjoy the vigorous activities of camp. Well, I didn't need the "talk" now. My last hazy thought was, *Will a bugle blast wake us up in the morning?* Then I sink once again into a dreamless sleep, happy my best friend is already snoring as sweetly as a saint!

Chapter 4

THE NAIL POLISH DISASTER

DAY TWO OF THE VACATION, AND I AM EVER SO HOPEFUL THAT today I will not be reminded of my former life back in the States. It's a new day in a new setting in a new country and so far, nothing reminds me of Marc. Hurrah!

Kim and I decide to get a spa service this morning. I make an appointment for a manicure and Kim for a facial. While we are walking over to the spa building, we come face to face with the biggest iguana I have ever seen. No joke, this guy is the size of a small alligator! He doesn't seem to be afraid of us in the least bit, so we tentatively pet him. He eyes us as if to say, "I own this place, so show me some respect." Sir Iggy, as we name him, really is regal, so we stand back, give him a little bow and move on.

When we get to the spa building I proceed upstairs to my manicure appointment. The cute little Mexican girl assigned to my manicure is doing her best to make small talk with me. Honestly, I think she is practicing her limited English more than she's socializing with me. *I know, I know, I'm being cynical. Damn, why does my mind seem determined to dwell on the negative?*

I'm not much into the conversation, though, because I am reminded of the manicures and massages I used to get while on vacation with Marc. *Shit, I can't go anywhere without thinking about him.* I fight back tears as hard as I can so I don't make her feel uncomfortable. I stare out the window so that she doesn't see my eyes.

Then the manicurist drops the bomb, "Are you here with your husband?"

A sob catches in my throat, then erupts and tears start streaming down my face.

My sweet, young manicurist tries to console me in her broken English, "So sorry, Missus. You okay?" *She must be wondering what she said wrong.*

I can only sputter and nod. And of course, I am not able to wipe the stream of tears away because my hands are both dipped in some pink, bubbly solution to soften my cuticles.

After what seems like a lifetime but is only a minute, I regain my composure long enough to get through what seems like the world's longest manicure. I am in such a hurry to get out of there, I actually bump into Kim as she is coming out of the facial room. If her expression mirrored mine, I must have looked like a person who just saw a ghost.

"I need to get out of here. Could you please take care of signing for the services? I wanna go back to the room."

"Sure, uh, wait for me outside."

When she joins me outside, tears are streaming down my face and she pleads, "What *happened* during your manicure?" I walk about twelve more steps, stop, look at my hands and start sobbing uncontrollably. "I… hate… this… nail… polish!"

Kim obviously must know that I am not sobbing over the color of my nail polish. But rather than having to hear for the one hundredth time that I think my life is over, she opts for silence. Not another word is spoken on the very long walk back to the hotel room. *Kim must be wishing she were back home—not two thousand miles away taking care of her friend who has totally cracked up.*

As we arrive at the hotel room, she uses her key to open the door and steps by to let me in. Alas, she is not home. She is in Mexico with me. That thought perks me up and suddenly grateful, I return to living in the present. As I step into our room and look at our view, I see, as if for the first time, a beautiful *balneario* with white sand beaches and aqua blue sea right in front of me. I feel like hugging her, but don't want to embarrass her. Actually it is I who feels embarrassed. *Holy cow, what a nutcase I can be.*

Chapter 5

ENTER THE CANADIANS

WE ARE BACK IN THE ROOM AND KIM IS STRETCHED OUT ON HER bed, all five-foot ten-inches of her, reading her magazines. I am lying on my bed feeling spent in the wake of the latest tsunami of tears, but gradually getting a grip on my thoughts. I do realize how utterly silly my little temper tantrum was about the color of my nail polish. Not only do I feel like my life sucks; now I am also making Kim's Christmas vacation suck by being such a crybaby about everything. *I have to do something to make her vacation good, but what? And how do I get out of myself long enough to do that?*

I have felt so totally out of control with my life and my emotions. It's weird—part of the time I am having an out of body experience, as if watching someone else live my life. Other times I am completely in my body, fully aware that my life is taking a dramatic change in direction. The part I hate the most, whether in or out of my body, is when I let myself succumb to the dark, sucking trap of negativity where I think my life has gone terribly wrong.

So what are you going to do about it? Sit around being a victim or take control of your life? Somehow, I don't think I'll get much sympathy, given that I am sitting in an all-inclusive resort on the beautiful beaches of the Riviera Maya. *Time to put on my big girl panties and reel in the out- of-control emotions.*

I take a deep breath and ask Kim in as cheerful a voice as I can manage, "So what are we going to do tonight?"

15

She looks up suddenly, watchful, then pleased. "I'm glad you asked. I've been looking through the visitor's guide and it looks like they have a club on the premises. Why don't we go check that out tonight?"

I've never really been to an all-inclusive resort before, so I'm up for trying it. And, the sheer physical toll the crying takes on my body is so depleting, sticking close to the room sounds good to me.

℘ ℘ ℘

About 7:00 p.m., we head to the Mexican food restaurant, Doña Maria's, on the premises of the resort. Kim knows that Mexican is my favorite kind of food, so if some real nachos and a margarita don't cheer me up, nothing will. The restaurant is decked out in all the traditional cantina décor (sombreros, Mexican flags, chili peppers, piñatas, and maracas). Sadly, it is a wasted opportunity, as I have yet to regain my appetite after two months. The good news is that for once in my adult life I am really happy with the way I look in a bikini. The bad news is I can't share this new smoking-hot body of mine with the only man I love. However, I am feeling a teensy bit more confident about meeting other guys now.

"You've got to eat more than that!" Kim says, watching me nibble on tiny nachos. "Three chips does not a meal make."

I shrug and try for one more but put it back on my plate and instead take a drink of my margarita.

After "dinner" we head over to the on-site night club about 8:00 p.m. There is almost nobody there. "So, where are all the hot guys you promised me?" I say to Kim.

"Just chill out, missy; it's a little early for the club scene down in Mexico. I'm sure some people will show up by 9:00," Kim reassures.

"Alright."

Then Kim waives the waiter over, "*Oye, masero, quieren dos margaritas, por favor.*"

I can't freakin' believe Kim's prediction! At 9:00 o'clock on the dot, a wave of Canadians (and not just any Canadians; some really cute, young, Canadians of the male variety) arrive on the scene. They see us, smile, and then after a quick animated huddle amongst themselves, approach our table. And we, of course, welcome them and their animal magnetism. There is nothing like the innate desire to be desired by the opposite sex to make it easy for a girl to flip a switch, which I now do. I am no longer, the shy, over-thinking, introverted girl with a traumatic loss; I'm a girl who puts on a happy face hoping to have fun.

Chapter 6

The "Aha" Moment

THERE IS NOT ONLY ONE WAVE OF CANADIANS, BUT TWO WAVES OF young, Canadian men ready to have fun. It's kind of funny how Kim is drawn more to the second group of Canadian guys and I favor the first group. *Oh, what the hell? Nothin' wrong with each of us having our own group of Canadians to hang out with!*

So, here I am in Playa del Carmen, Mexico, sitting at a table amongst my seven new best friends from Canada, doing shots. Shots of what, you may be wondering? Not all shots are the same—there are shots of tequila, shots of schnapps, Jell-O shots and many more. On this particularly festive evening, my new friends have chosen to imbibe Jägermeister shots. Now I've done a few shots in my thirty-nine years, but never Jägermeister shots. I am curious about them and there's only one way to learn. "*Masero, yo quiero una mas round of Jägermeister shots para mis amigos!*"

One of the quieter Canadians with John Lennon glasses and the cutest, shyest smile tells me all about this drink new to me. He says, "The word Jägermeister means a master hunter and it was made originally as a digestif and a cough remedy."

"Yes, Mr. Wikipedia," says his very buff Canadian friend, who towers over everybody even sitting down at the table.

"It does kind of cough like smell syrup," I say.

Everyone stares at me for a second, frowning.

"What, what did I say?"

John Lennon Glasses says, "You mean 'it smells like cough syrup,' right?"

"Yes, that's what I said."

Everyone laughs and I realize that I've mixed up my words again, like I do more than I want to admit.

John Lennon Glasses continues his lecture, apparently trying to impress me with his knowledge. "Jägermeister is a type of liqueur made with over sixty ingredients."

"Do tell, Wiki," another friend jokes.

"Technically speaking, Jägermeister has fifty-six herbs, fruits, roots and spices including citrus peel, licorice, anise, poppy seeds, saffron, ginger, juniper berries and ginseng."

"You're a fruit!" the buff Canadian cuts him off and the other guys laugh. "Hey, drink up, boys and girls," someone says.

"To roots and fruits," someone else adds. And we do. I realize these guys are way younger than us, but who cares, they are fun and nice.

Kim, being ever so protective of her newly single and very naïve friend, is keeping a watchful eye on me. She and her new best friends are now hanging out on the swings. There are many swings in Mexico at the bars. I'm not exactly sure why that is. However, I must confess there is something very young, fun and whimsical about sitting on a swing, drinking a frou-frou drink with a little umbrella in it. These boys are such a welcome relief to the heaviness I have been living. They come to us at the exact right time.

All the great life-coaching gurus say that having fun is good for the soul! So, there, I'm doing it!

It sure doesn't hurt either, that the boys are in shock that I am thirty-nine going on forty. Still being rather naïve, I am not sure if this is a line that guys use on all middle-aged women or not. Whether it is for real or just a pick-up line, I don't care. It's working. I love being chatted-up by a bunch of twenty and thirty-somethings, as if I'm the greatest thing since the Internet. Never mind that there are not any other single ladies in the club. Tonight, this club is *mine*! I am that fun person I used to be in college and I am going to eat this up—every single moment of it!

∿ ∿ ∿

Later on that night I scoot my chair closer to John Lennon Glasses and ask, "Why do you know so much about drinks?" I gaze in his eyes like this is the most fascinating topic I've ever talked about, hoping he might get the hint and kiss me.

"I like to study the culture behind food and beverages. Weird, right?"

"Not at all. I think your useless facts are very interesting."

"Well, Jaegermeister is especially interesting."

I lean towards him with an encouraging look, willing him to kiss me. But no, he's more interested in launching into his lecture again.

"I forgot to tell you this. The ingredients are ground, and then steeped in water and alcohol for a few days. See, then they filter the mixture and store it in oak barrels for about a year."

I nod, blinking my eyes in wonderment.

"When a year has passed, the liqueur is filtered again, and then mixed with water, alcohol and sugar and I can't remember the other thing. Oh yeah, caramel! I mean they go to a lot of trouble to put smiles on our faces."

"Ummm yummy," I purr, then sing-song, "And it's good for you, too!"

We both laugh and then he gives me that sweet, shy smile. What I really want is a sweet, shy kiss. Oh well, perhaps in due time. I like him. *Hey, I like guys again! And having fun is waaaay better than not having fun,* I think, smiling at my childlike revelation.

Chapter 7

NARCISSISM: NOT A BEACH TOPIC

"UGGGGGGH! KIM! WHY DIDN'T YOU STOP ME??"

"Oh, no! No way was I going to stop you from the first time you actually got out of your head, let loose and had a little fun since that dreadful day. Un, uh. No way."

"Okay, so did I pass step one of Kim's 'love rehab program' for me?"

"Yes, Pal, with flying colors!"

Man, I keep forgetting that the downside to having *that* much fun on any given evening comes with a price. And that price today is a big, hairy, hangover. "Okay, but don't expect much intellectual conversation today. What can we do today that does not involve my brain or much of my body either, for that matter?"

"Let's get in some beach time. Surely, you can make your way to a lounging chair where you can get horizontal again."

"I dunno, but I'll give it a try."

So, we pack up our iPods, reading material, sunscreen, sunglasses, beach towels and water bottles and head out. As we walk down to the beach, we pass some workers planting palm trees and other various tropical flora on the property.

Kim tells me that Playa del Carmen got hit by two Category 4 hurricanes earlier this year—Hurricane Emily in July and Hurricane

Wilma in October. "All people really talk about back home, though, is Hurricane Katrina because of how badly she devastated New Orleans. But here, the entire resort property is still recovering from Hurricane Wilma," Kim says.

I remember the front desk gal telling us that all the beachfront rooms had to be gutted and completely overhauled, "which is why we do not have any beachfront rooms available at this time." *Likely story,* I had thought, skeptical of her excuse, but way back then (three days ago) I didn't know about Wilma. Plus I was so much more cynical before the Canadians!

Nearly to the beach, we befriend one of the resort staff, as we often do, thanks to Kim's outgoing personality. "*Hola, buenos dias,*" Kim says to the cute Latino who seems to be in charge.

"*Hola,*" the guy replies back to us. The staff here is so friendly. I wonder if it's genuine or if they are paid to be friendly to us. I catch myself and check my cynicism again. No matter. It's fun to interact with them, regardless of their motives.

It gives me and Kim a chance to practice our Spanglish. Okay, hers is pretty damn good, so I'll call it Spanish. Mine is way more English than Spanish. I guess that makes our average Spanglish! "*¿Como se llama, amigo?*" Kim asks.

"Lalo."

"*Hola, Lalo. ¿Qué pasa?*" asking them what they are doing.

"You want the English or the Spanish version?" Lalo asks.

Kim's face reddens a bit.

"English, please," I chime in.

"We are replacing all the trees and flora that Hurricane Wilma destroyed," he said.

"Bummer."

"Yes, I am normally the entertainment director for the resort. However, today I am directing employees where to place the new trees and flora for the grounds. All resort employees get re-deployed to prepare for a hurricane and to clean-up after a hurricane—cooks, reception staff, entertainers, managers—everyone."

"What kind of entertainment do you direct?" Kim asks Lalo.

"We do a traditional folk show, with Mexican singing and dancing. It is very good. We involve the audience. It is a lot of fun. I am the emcee. You should come tonight."

"What's that?" I ask Lalo, pointing to what looks like a large palm tree enwrapped in a burlap sheath that looks like a tree condom.

"Oh, that is the way we transport mature palm trees so that the fronds do not get damaged during transport. They are very fragile, you know."

"Interesting." My attention span is about five seconds because all I can think about right now is laying down my throbbing head on a beach chair. "Well, *mucho gusto*, Lalo," I say.

"*Hasta luego*!" Kim and I say in unison and carry on towards our beach destination.

We find our perfect lounge chairs, face them directly towards the sun to get a perfectly even tan, place our towels with perfect alignment for our head and feet and promptly settle into our books. Kim has chosen *Marley and Me* for her beach reading and I have brought the seven hundred page tome on, yup, you guessed it, *Narcissism*. You can imagine what a barrel of laughs we were at the beach, Kim with her tear-jerker and me with a book on the symptoms, risk factors and treatments of personality disorders!

After about an hour of this glum reading, Kim is crying into her beach towel again, when we spot John Lennon Glasses, the cute Canadian, be-bopping down the beach towards us. He really is cute, even without my "beer goggles" on, albeit a little young. But Kim keeps telling me I need a boy-toy to help me get over what's-his-name. So, maybe he's it!

John Lennon Glasses sits down on the edge of my lounge chair, and his suntan lotion smells good. He smells yummy. "Hey, what are you ladies up to today?"

"We're recovering from a very long evening with some wild and crazy Canadians," I say, forcing myself to sound cheerful.

"Ahhh, that was so much fun last night," he sighs. "So, whatcha reading, Brooke?"

"Er, uh, well, it's a book on narcissism," I sputter.

"What?"

"Yeah, just a topic I wanted to do some research on while I had some down time."

"Oh, are you a psychiatrist or something?"

"No, I told you last night I am a Denver Broncos cheerleader."

"Oh, riiiiight, I forgot. No, seriously. Why, narcissism?"

"Oh, it's a long story you don't wanna hear."

"You're probably right…Hey, well, I gotta run. I'll catch you ladies, later." And off he goes, just as quickly as he arrived. *I wonder why he ran off so fast. Surely it has nothing to do with my chosen reading material?*

I look down at my tome. It's making welts in my legs it's so heavy, literally and figuratively. It makes me feel miserable and hopeless. I get up, take the book with me and dump it into the wire trash can. And with that singular, spectacular act, I have taken a huge weight off my mind.

Chapter 8

WHY YOU NO SCREAM "VIVA?!"

TONIGHT, WE'RE STILL DRAGGING A LITTLE (OKAY, WE'RE DRAGGING a lot) and decide to stay on the premises of the all-inclusive resort.

"What can we do with the least amount of effort and still be able to say we did something?" I ask Kim.

"I know what we should do. Lalo said they were having a pretty good show tonight. Let's go check it out."

"Perfect!" I'm only steps away from the room should I suddenly decide I've had enough fun for one day and need to turn in early—which is a distinct possibility because of the vice-like grip my hangover still has on my body.

ॐ ॐ ॐ

Lalo is here tonight, as promised, directing the show. He looks like he's right out of a Mexican TV game show. He's got that funny dorsal fin-looking spiked haircut that is really popular with young Hispanic guys. Oddly enough, the dorsal fin look actually works for him. He's also got the thick-rimmed, low-profile GQ glasses. Lalo is impeccably dressed in his entertainment director's uniform: white resort-wear slacks, white loafers, lime green button down shirt and a slightly darker green tie. He's got the dark, liquid Latin eyes and very dark sun-kissed skin, which of

27

course makes his teeth look especially pearly white. He also has a very large, non-offensive tiger tattoo on his left forearm, which gives him a bad-boy air. His only physical fault, if he has one, is that he's a little vertically-challenged. But that does not detract from his overall charm.

The entertainment director's primary job (as far as I can tell) is to entertain the audience before the show and during the intermission. He's doing his best to liven up this slightly lackluster crowd. Maybe they're all hungover like me.

Lalo says "We're going to play a little game. Okay? Everyone up for that?"

"Sure," we mumble.

"We're going to see which side of the room is better at our little game. Okay?"

What better way to liven up a crowd than to incite a little friendly competition?

Lalo instructs one side of the room to join him in yelling out, "*Viva*" and the other side of the room to join him in saying, "Mexico." The two words together will mean, "long live Mexico." With an overly dramatic lunge of his body, he cues: "*Viva;*" then lunging toward the other side, he cues: "Mexico;" Lunge—"*Viva,*" Lunge—"Mexico," "*Viva,*" "Mexico," "*Viva,*" "Mexico." After about the fifth time, our enthusiasm begins to wane, and when he cues the sixth time to say "*Viva,*" he practically gets silence.

He stops dead in his tracks and in a pleading voice says: "Why you no scream '*Viva*'???"

The disappointed, distraught look on his face, combined with his Mexican accent and broken English, is hysterical and Kim and I laugh until tears come to our eyes.

The best phrase of the whole vacation is born. Thank you, Lalo.

From now on during our trip and even beyond, if either of us starts acting sad or grumpy or gets too serious, we use this to poke fun at each other: "Why you no scream '*viva*'?" It cracks us up every time.

The show turns out, in fact, to be entertaining in a folksy sort of way. And just when we think the evening is over, Lalo and some of his buddies from the show come and join us at our table. We seem to be a magnet for young, cute, single guys this trip—must be sending out a beacon signal of some sort. I've heard about this before; however, having been part of a couple for all of my twenties and thirties, I have not experienced it before this trip.

Kim has been saying, over and over that I really have to stop taking myself so seriously and I'm now beginning to see what she means. I have to admit, I go into serious mode a lot of the time when I'm scared or insecure. Okay, step two of Kim's love rehab program must be: "Don't take life so seriously," And I finally get it. *Why you no scream 'viva'?*

Chapter 9

Lesbian Couples Massage

"**H**APPY BIRTHDAY, KIM!"

"Thanks and Merry Christmas to you." Kim is a Christmas baby and I resolve to make this the best birthday she's ever had after all she's doing for me.

"Well, Birthday Girl, what should we do on this festive day in paradise?"

Kim looks so relieved when I'm cheerful like this. "Let's treat ourselves to a massage."

"Great idea!" I say. "I haven't had a massage in forever. I'll call and make us both an appointment. How does 11:00 o'clock sound?"

"Perfect. A nice leisurely breakfast, then a nice leisurely massage, a little beach time, then let's head into the town of Playa and check out what's going on in town. That would be a perfect birthday, in my book."

"Your wish is my command!" I chuckle.

We head down to the resort's main dining room for their daily breakfast buffet. I just love breakfast in a foreign country. It's not the typical bacon, eggs, pancakes, fruit, cereal, Danish and juice from frozen concentrate that you would find at an American hotel's breakfast buffet. No, they usually have a spread that includes meats, cheeses, rolls, freshly squeezed fruit juices and some local delicacy. Always, always, the juice is squeezed fresh. In some foreign countries, the bonus local delicacy could include pickled fish, pork-filled pancakes, bird's nest soup, mashed fava beans, feta on lavash, or bread with peanut butter, cheese and chocolate on the same slice. Mmmm… yum! In Mexico, the local delicacy includes *Chilaquiles*. OMG—I think I've died and gone to heaven. All my favorite foods combined into one creamy dish of luvin' goodness. *Chilaquiles* are lightly fried corn tortillas, topped with scrambled eggs, pulled chicken, *queso fresco* and *crema*, swimming in salsa. *Queso fresco* translates to "fresh cheese" and has a crumbly texture and slightly acidic flavor, kind of like Feta cheese. *Crema*, a dairy staple in Mexican cuisine, is not a cheese but a heavy cream that would remind you of *crème fraîche* or sour cream.

Did I mention, I think I've died and gone to heaven? This might be the first time in two months that I've actually had an appetite for anything. But the *Chilaquiles*… now we're talking!

After scarfing down a half plate of these delectable morsels, I say to Kim, "Surely, step three of your love rehab program is: Don't stop eating when you're sad. Fall in love with food again."

"Why do you keep saying that? This ain't no rehab program, Pal. This trip is just about us having a good time and if I can help in any way, terrific. However, I do love seeing you eat!"

"Well, today is your day and I want to help you celebrate it big time. Let's go have our massages."

On the way over to the spa, I entertain Kim with my massage stories.

"One time in Cuomo, Italy, I received a massage from this gorgeous Italian masseur dressed in his tight-white spa uniform which still couldn't hide his sculpted biceps and perfectly shaped glutes. I could hardly understand a word he said. But when he asked if I wanted him to massage my belly, I miraculously understood him enough to say 'uh, yes, please.' And let me tell you, Kim, if you ever find yourself in Italy and a gorgeous Italian masseur asks you if you want your belly massaged, do not pass up the invitation! You will not regret it."

"Don't worry about it, I'm there."

"You will love my other massage story. One time Marc and I took a cruise along the Vietnam coast. We did an overnight excursion to Hanoi and while there, I got a massage from a young Vietnamese girl, and it was the exact opposite experience. For the first half of the massage, she was on her cell phone with her boyfriend, holding the phone with one hand and barely rubbing my arm with her other hand. And if that wasn't bad enough, when she finished the call with her boyfriend, she said to me, 'Miss Brooke, I like to luk you.'"

I said "Pardon me, what?"

"I like to luk you."

"What?"

"I like to luk you."

"I had no idea if she was saying she liked to look at me or if she wanted to lick me. All I know is I couldn't get off that table fast enough because neither one appealed to me!"

Kim is buckled over she's laughing so hard. It's nice I can make her laugh for a change.

We check in at the spa's reception desk and after a short wait, a woman comes to get both Kim and I, to take us back to our massages. I think it's a little odd that the same woman is taking us both back to our massage rooms. Usually your massage therapist comes and takes you to his or her designated room. But for some reason this woman is walking us back to our rooms together.

We get to the room and she waves us both to go inside the *same* room. Can you believe my horror when I enter and find two tables set up side-by-side for us to get a "couples massage?" I mean, I know the resort's target clientele is couples and honeymooners. But, c'mon. *Really*?

Once we get past the shock of the situation, we buck up and have our "couples massage." I hasten to add that there is no eroticism involved. But we giggle throughout the massage. At one point, Kim can hardly get the words out she's laughing so hard but I finally understand her. She says, "Miss Brooke, I really want to luk you."

I scream with laughter and say, "Come to think of it, Kim, you have been a rather perfect date on our Mexican adventure." And we crack up some more.

Chapter 10

¿POR QUÉ NO?

KIM AND I GET DRESSED AND HEAD BACK TO OUR HOTEL ROOM after our first and *last* "couples massage." After laughing hysterically for an hour about the whole mix-up, the romantic music they played, the baffled looks on the faces of the massage therapists when we were cracking up so much we were rolled up holding our stomachs. We were not being very cooperative and peaceful clients.

% % %

We finally make our plans for the evening.

"Where would you like to go for dinner?" I ask Kim as we're riding the hotel shuttle into town.

"I don't know. Let's just walk down Fifth Avenue and stop wherever our noses take us."

"Sounds good to me."

We are walking down Fifth Avenue and being accosted by what seems like every store vendor on the street. "Hey, beautiful ladies. I have a special bargain just for you."

"No, *gracias*."

"You want a Mexican boyfriend?"

"No, *gracias*."

"Why not?"

"No, *gracias.*"

And so it goes, all the way down Fifth Avenue. We run across a cute little cantina named, "The Tequila Barrel," where it looks like they serve gigantic margaritas and where Christmas revelers are laughing and singing—wrapped in a merry, festive mood. I suggest to Kim that we stop there for a little pre-dinner aperitif.

"*¿Por qué no?*" she replies.

We belly-up to the bar and order two large margaritas, because it is, after all, Kim's birthday and the happy atmosphere in this place is infectious—Kim is grinning ear-to-ear! I think the large margaritas must be thirty-two ounces. No joke. I know I can handle it, though. But apparently Kim doesn't think I can, for she says, "Uh, Brooke, you need to eat something so you don't drown in that margarita."

"I did. I ate some nachos, it's plenty," I say.

"You ate two triangles, I watched you. That is not *food*," Kim says, a concerned look on her face.

I chuckle and point out some colorful characters walking down Fifth Avenue towards us. As it turns out, this is the perfect place to people watch.

A group of young Latinos come by and stop in front of The Tequila Barrel. They start performing street break-dancing, which is amazing: twirling on their backs, doing flips and snaking their torsos. Some of them jump up high using athletic leaps and then twist into undulating moves again. Around the periphery of the dancers are little kids selling somewhat wilted flowers they've probably found discarded at the local flower shops. I feel expansive and buy some, giving them to Kim who looks pleased even while laughing as the flowers flop over in her hand.

We are enthralled. "Let's have another round of margaritas," I tell Kim.

"*¿Por qué no?*" she replies. Kim is feeling more festive than usual today. I love that I am able to instigate a good time.

After leaving The Tequila Barrel, we come across La Parilla (which means The Grill) in our search for the perfect birthday dinner location. The place smells of rotisserie chicken—so delectable. Picture the cartoon where the character is lifted off his feet and drawn by his nose into the aroma wafting from the eatery—that is us. We hold onto the railings to balance our tipsy selves as we climb the stairs to the upstairs dining area.

I'm sitting with my back to the bar and bartender and Kim is facing them. Because of the weight I have lost recently, all my clothes are practically hanging off of me, including the pants I am wearing tonight. The bartender and his friend start giggling and pointing at me.

In Spanish, Kim asks the bartender, "What is so funny, my friend?"

The two of them talk at once, "We can see your friend's pretty peach-colored undergarment and we would like to be given her panties, please."

What?!? Kim translates to me and I immediately feel my face flush and wriggle in my seat trying to pull up the waistband of my pants.

When they bring us our food—melt-in-your-mouth chicken, beans and rice—which we devour, the amused waiter chimes in, "It is a Christmas tradition. There is a wall in the back room where we hang the underwear of pretty patrons. Would you pretty ladies like to honor our tradition?"

"But, this is her birthday!" I say, between bites of succulent chicken, as if that would change the subject.

Oh God; now I've opened another can of worms. Next thing I know, they send over a complimentary Sex on the Beach drink for her birthday and in honor of my peach panties, since it happens to have peach schnapps in it. With as straight a face as he can muster, our waiter tells us about yet another tradition.

"It is customary on someone's birthday, that the birthday lady and her female companion give all the waiters a kiss and a hug."

Kim and I throw up our hands in resignation and start to laugh. *¿Por qué no?* And in an instant, the waiters, all ten of them working the upstairs dining room, line up and give both Kim and I a hug and a kiss on one cheek, as is customary in Mexican culture.

During all these shenanigans we somehow have consumed our food, the birthday drinks and sixty-four ounces of Margaritas each. We decide it is time to *vamanos*. We plunk down some money for our food and drinks and totter down two sets of stairs to the *baños* to visit the ladies' room before we leave.

We are having a jolly time, very happy to be relieving our full bladders. Suddenly I get serious and ask Kim, "So, do we give our underwear to them?"

Kim replies, "I don't know; I've never had such a request before!"

We both snort with laughter, while I try to picture my underwear hanging in the unlikely room. Then I suddenly announce, "I'm gonna do it. I'm giving them my underwear. *¿Por qué no?*"

"You're going to give them your fifty-dollar La Perla lingerie that you just bought?"

"Only the best for their panty gallery!" I snort again.

"Okay, I'm in. *¿Por qué no?*" Kim declares with a brave voice.

Kim and I convulse with laughter and then, locking the bathroom door, disrobe, remove and wad up our panties. Once dressed again, this time minus underwear, we start up the stairs with the prized panties bundled up in our hands. Waiting at the top of the stairs is our grinning waiter. Without a word, he holds out the pockets of his apron signaling where to place our panties. *How did he know we would do this? We are so subtle and lady-like!*

We quickly deposit our panties in his apron pockets, so as not to be noticed. No such luck. As we try to make our escape, we look up and see all nine of the other waiters applauding and cheering us on. So much for discretion.

[Author's Note: Not a single Mexican I have ever talked to since then was familiar with either the kissing/hugging birthday "tradition" or the Christmas panty donation "tradition." Hmmmm, think we were duped?]

Chapter 11

THE BLUE PARROT

"OH, MY GOD, KIM, I CANNOT BELIEVE WE JUST DID THAT," I SAY as we scurry out of La Parilla and into the street.

Kim replies, "And I'm wearing a short dress. I mean, any little breeze… at least you're wearing pants."

I burst out laughing looking at her holding down her skirt.

She adds, "Well, that will certainly go on the bucket list and immediately get crossed off."

"With a big black Sharpie pen, right?"

"Jumbo sized."

"Think maybe we went too far?"

"Nah. One thing I admire about you, Brooke, is that when you do something, you go for it all the way. I'm a little in awe, actually. But my privates are feeling a little too exposed right now, that's all."

I giggle. "C'mon, walk fast before any of the waiters decide to follow us."

"Oh, yeah, that *is* a possibility, isn't it!"

"So, where to now, birthday girl?" I ask, still giggling, since we are just cracking ourselves up.

"Since this is the birthday I will remember for doing daring things, let's just keep walking down Fifth Avenue again and see what other trouble we can get into."

I love Kim for enjoying our escapade; she looks young, flushed and happy. "Oh, wait, look. Let's go down this street. Looks like there are some bars down there that are hoppin'."

"I heard that the Blue Parrot has a fire show of some sort. Why don't we see if we can catch it?" she says.

"Well, now that sounds a little dangerous. I'm in!"

We plunge forward toward our next adventure.

% % %

The Blue Parrot has swings everywhere. I love how fun and playful that makes me feel. And it has the dance floor and DJ right on the beach under the stars.

"Oh my gosh, Kim, look at the ground. This bar is built right on the beach. In the words of Toby Keith, 'I love this bar!'"

We both immediately ditch our shoes and bury our toes into the cool, soft sand. Ooh, the sand feels so good between my toes. Especially because these are not the most comfortable sandals I've ever worn. The sand feels like a spa treatment on my feet.

We make our way over to the fire show that's in progress. "Holy cow, Kim, look at that! These performers are amazing!"

On stage are these young, fit Latinos, juggling fire in the most sensual display of acrobatics I've ever seen. I notice Kim keeps smoothing her skirt down, unconsciously. It makes me smile all over again each time, but she's totally engrossed in the show. Afterwards, a young guy comes up to me and whisks me into his arms and onto the dance floor before I have a chance to say anything to him or Kim and in a few seconds, we are lost in a sea of dancers crowding the dance floor.

After a couple of dances, Kim wedges herself onto the dance floor, takes my arm and pulls me off the dance floor. "Hey, Brooke, aren't those the crazy Canadians we were hanging out with at our resort the other night?"

"Yeah, it is. Let's go say hi."

We sashay over to the Canadians. They light up like just-plugged-in Christmas trees and give some cheers and high-fives when we join them. They tell us that they left our resort and checked into a hotel just a block away in the heart of Playa, saying that they need more action, stimulation and excitement. *Yeah, I'll bet!* They also tell us that we are the most fun and interesting single ladies they've met. *Uh huh!*

"So what have you ladies been up to on this festive Christmas evening?"

"Well, as a matter of fact, it is Kim's birthday today and we spent Happy Hour at The Tequila Barrel and then dinner at La Parilla, where we learned of a Mexican tradition for ladies who have birthdays on Christmas."

"Oh yeah, what was that?"

"Well, it seems as though the waiters provide hugs and kisses to all the ladies in the birthday party."

"That sounds bogus," one of the Canadians says.

"Not only that…" and now I look at Kim to see if it's okay to disclose the next part.

She nods, I think. So I continue, "And then you leave your underwear for them to put on their 'wall of fame.'"

"What? No way," the second Canadian exclaims.

"Way," I say, for some reason proud of this idiotic act.

"Seriously, you gave them your underwear?" Canadian number one says.

I glance at Kim and she admits, "Yup." But she doesn't look all that proud of our idiotic act.

"I would have loved to have seen that."

"Indeed; it was a riot *and* a once-in-a-lifetime event," Kim says.

One of the Canadians gives me a look that says, "This woman may be the hottie I'd like to spend some time with… starting right now!"

"Hey, you ladies want to dance?" he says.

"Absolutely!" we say, and the towering Canadian guy giving me "the look" gets to me first, pulling me onto the dance floor.

We are gettin' our boogie on when my oversized, crazy Canadian dancing partner shouts over the loud techno, disco sounds so popular with the young scene in Mexico, "You look really festive in that pink color. What do they call that color, fuchsia or magenta or something like that?"

I nod, all grins, twirls and swirls.

He continues to shout, "It looks good with the bling on your back pockets."

Then, all the sudden my crazy Canadian dancing partner manages to slip his hands down the back side of my too-big pants and stops dead in his tracks. "Holy shit, you weren't kidding about giving away your panties!"

I too have stopped dead in my tracks, smoothly removing his hands from my backside and replying, "Now, would I kid about a thing like that!"

Meanwhile, Kim comes over and tells me that her dancing partner is working another angle. She said he told her that there's a Canadian tradition that girls with birthdays on Christmas go home with the cutest Canadian guys in the club. We giggle and she asks, "What do ya think?" And then she smoothes down her skirt.

Although I would like to get that first post break-up "male encounter" under my belt, I don't think I'm quite ready for it. Kim has several times told me I need to "get back in the saddle" soon. She has said it is vitally important to my healing to feel like a desirable, lovable woman again.

I'm not sure I'm a one-night-stand kind of gal, though. I'm no angel, mind you. I've had my share of dalliances in my youth. However, I'm almost forty years old now and I'm just not sure that is the life I want to create for myself. Then again, I never thought in a million years, I'd give my fifty dollar peach-colored thong panties to a waiter named José in a restaurant in Mexico either! And that felt oddly liberating. *Hmmm, maybe I do want to live a little and take more risks in life. It's not hurting anybody. Risks? Okay, maybe, but tonight's not the night. I am a little tipsy and don't feel like that's a safe thing to do.*

After rejecting the guys' proposition, Kim decides we've probably had enough alcohol and merry-making for this birthday and calls it an evening. We say our goodbyes, make our way to the exit, pour ourselves into one of the many cabs waiting outside the club and go back to the safety of our all-inclusive resort, miles away from the crazy Canadians. On the drive home, the cab driver is speeding, now and then lurching the car forward, careening around curves.

Kim asks me, "Are you okay, I hope you aren't going to get sick?"

I laugh. "Of course not." I put my head back on the seat and instantly fall asleep.

At one point the cab shrieks to a stop. I awake. "Hey what's going on?" I ask, completely lucid.

"It's some kind of a checkpoint." Kim says. "We'll be home soon."

❧ ❧ ❧

The next thing I know, I'm waking up and strangely, I can see everything very clearly in our hotel room. I'm thinking I've had some sort of spiritual awakening with the events of last night and I am seeing the world more clearly now. And then I realize that, nope, I've slept in my contacts all night and now they are completely stuck to my eyeballs. This is not good. And neither is the fact that I slept in my fuchsia pink top and black pants with the sequined pockets. Kim tells me she's impressed with the amount of alcohol I can apparently drink without getting sick or out of control.

"Who knew such a small person could handle her alcohol so well," Kim says.

While graciously accepting her compliment (I think)... I'm privately musing, *why, why, why did I have to have that one last margarita?*

Chapter 12

Home Sweet Home

AFTER BUCKLING UP AND SETTLING IN WITH MY *Us Weekly* MAGA-zine, I turn to Kim. "Thank God we're on a much nicer plane for the trip home. It doesn't seem like a cattle car at all. Is this a different airline?"

Kim says, "Nope, same airline, same plane; it's *you* who is different, Pal. I'm flying home with a different Brooke than the woman I flew to Playa with."

Indeed, I am. I feel much lighter emotionally, much more at ease, more hopeful. Ready to face the world and ready to jump back into my real life. "So, Kim, you know how you've been telling me I need to get back in the saddle and start dating again? I think I'm ready, but how does one find a guy to date these days? Other than in wild bars in Mexico."

"Well, first you need to define the type of guy you are looking for before you go looking for him. You gotta have 'the list.'"

"'The list?' Oh, okay, how do I get that? I feel so stupid having to ask you all these questions; but seriously, I have not been on the dating scene in twenty years and I think I've forgotten how."

"It really is a different dating world these days. I've been through it, I figured it out. You need 'the list.'"

I must give her another blank look.

"Okay, think fast, what are the top ten qualities you are looking for in a man? No, wait; let's start with the deal-killers."

"Oh, that's easy," I say. "My top deal-killer is *no hunters*. My ex-husband was a hunter and I hate that he enjoyed killing animals for sport. I'm mortified that I even went with him on hunts."

"What? You actually hunted? I can't imagine you wearing camouflage and carrying a rifle looking for Bambi. You're such a huge animal lover and so girly."

"I know, right? And even stranger than that, just imagine me carrying a bow and arrow."

"You did? Now, you're pulling my leg."

"Nope. Thinking back, I'm shocked at how much I compromised for that man." For a second I ponder this. *Do other women change who they are to be acceptable or loved by some guy? Or am I the only one? It really reflected my lack of self-esteem or self-identity at that point in my life. Or perhaps it was just a limited knowledge of self.*

"Okay, moving on, then," Kim interrupts my thoughts. "So, what is your top must-have in a man?"

"Hmmm… that's a little harder. On the one hand, I would like someone who's loyal, loving and handsome. On the other hand, I'd like someone who's adventurous, exciting and wealthy. Is that unrealistic? *Probably.* What's the most important quality on your list?"

"Sense of humor, without a doubt. Not having one is absolutely a deal breaker. I do not want any guy who takes himself or life in general too seriously. Must love dogs, too. I'm a package deal. And he can't 'fake-like' my dogs, he has to really love 'em."

"You know, I'm really glad we didn't go home with the crazy Canadians," I tell Kim.

"What makes you say that?"

"Well, although I'm all for getting that first love encounter under my belt, I would really like to find another long-term partner. I don't think I'm cut out for one-night stands."

"Yeah, me neither." Kim says. "The good news is, *you* decide. *You* get to decide who you want to spend your time with. It's liberating!"

"Yeah, I guess starting over is not all that bad." I say.

"Yay!" She high-fives me. "By the way, this trip's been good for me, too. Those Crazy Canadians were fun, but I'm really looking for more than that… I can't help myself; I like to fall in love."

"You're a hopeless romantic! Nothing wrong with that."

We both sigh. "Well, I'm officially exhausted; even *thinking* about what I want in a male partner gives me brain fatigue!" Then I announce, "I'm going to take a nap."

"Yeah, me too!"

%   %   %

I awake from a very different sleep than the hung over-sickish nap I took on the trip down. I wait until Kim wakes up and then, we are both quiet a while, looking out the window at the clouds gliding by. I finally break the silence, "You know, this trip was really different from my trips with Marc. With him, we did the same routine every day: go to the pool, get a massage, eat dinner, go to bed. With us… well, we are more spontaneous. And that's new for me. I love it."

"That makes me very happy, Brooke."

"And, Kim, you were amazing to me, this trip, really, I'm going to have to call you Saint Kim from now on, after all you've gotten me through."

She laughs. "I ain't no saint, but I like being your pal."

%   %   %

After warm hugs outside my rental house, I wave good-bye to Kim as she drives off. As I roll my luggage up to my door, I contemplate how our getaway was the perfect escape from my imperfect life, *and* I am glad to be home, imperfect life and all. I can hardly wait to see my dogs, *and* I look forward to moving into my new permanent home in a few months, once construction has been completed. *That's a refreshing perspective—I'm living in the world of "and." Perhaps my cynicism is fading away. It's about damn time!*

WHY YOU NO SCREAM VIVA?!

As I close the front door, I sigh and look around at my new transition home. A chill runs through my body as I realize, *It is possible to start over and create a life with some joy and adventure. Here I go!*

PART TWO

Finding My Healing Place –
Hello Maya!

୬ ୬ ୬

I am not what happened to me;
I am what I choose to become.

~ Carl Jung ~

Chapter 13

CHICHÉN ITZÁ MAGIC

WIKIPEDIA DEFINES "PERFECT STORM" AS AN EXPRESSION THAT describes an event where a rare combination of circumstances will aggravate a situation drastically. That's my life exactly: a perfect storm of life events. Not only did I lose the man I thought I'd spend the rest of my life with in October, but as I've mentioned, I will turn forty in January. The third blow occurs when my boss informs me of an impending merger and the company I work for will be moving to North Carolina. I'm offered a transfer but don't want to move there. By July, I'm without a job.

So, what's a girl to do? Yup, get my butt back to Playa, where so much magic and transformation occurred last Christmas. After all, I'm "free" now, except for a few loose ends. Playa seems to be calling out to me for more healing adventures. Luckily, my partner-in-crime, Kim, is up for more shenanigans.

This trip we want to stay closer to town, like the Crazy Canadians had done. In addition, after our "couples massage" experience at the couples/honeymooners resort, we pick a family-friendly 5-star all-inclusive resort, the Iberostar Tucán, in the gated community of Playacar—a bedroom community to Playa del Carmen.

Upon arrival, we are greeted by a band of coatis. These funny little creatures are about the size of a large cat and look like they might belong to the raccoon family. Their tails are as long as their bodies, which helps them balance as they stand up to beg for food. I've heard raccoons can be mean, so I keep my distance from them, even though they sure are cute.

The resort is decorated in traditional bright Mexican colors, with splashes of yellow, blue and red everywhere. Most of the buildings have the typical thatched roofs made from the fronds of palm trees. Yellow lounge chairs dot the extensive private beach. There is a heavy influence of Mayan culture and symbolism throughout the property. The lobby is appointed with carved friezes and colorful murals depicting gods and other mythological creatures of some sort. There are mini temples with stepped pyramids strategically built into the architecture throughout the property. Our room is accented with beautiful cotton textiles, probably handcrafted by Mayan artisans. And what Mayan-influenced resort would be complete without the circular ceramic Mayan calendar everywhere?

While we are definitely closer to town than we were at El Dorado Royale, it is still about a ten to fifteen minute walk to get to where all the action is in Playa del Carmen. It's lovely here, but I'm beginning to feel that the magic I seek is found outside the resort—in the real Playa…or beyond. Spurred by that feeling, we decide to go in search of the ancient magic of the Chichén Itzá Ruins.

℀ ℀ ℀

"How long do you think this bus ride is to Chichén Itzá?" I ask Kim as we settle into our tour bus.

"The tour guide said it's about three hours."

"So how about a little Mayan history while we have the time?"

"Bring it on."

I pull out the brochure the tour guide gave us and begin reading to Kim after the bus takes off: "Chichén Itzá was named one of the seven wonders of the current world in 2007. Nearly ninety million people voted online to determine the world's top seven human-built wonders, also including the Great Wall of China, Petra in Jordan, Brazil's statue of Christ the Redeemer, Peru's Machu Picchu, the Colosseum in Rome and India's Taj Mahal."

I read for quite a while and when I glance over at Kim, she's snoozing. Ha, ha, so much for my history lesson. I decide to take a little nap too. I've been dozing a lot this trip. Dreaming, for me, is part healing and part revealing.

%% %% %%

I dream that we are on a local bus, not a tour bus filled with middle-class, white people from all-inclusive resorts. In the dream, the brown man and woman in the seats across the aisle are holding three kids and two chickens. The well-behaved children look at us with dark, soulful eyes. The chickens' heads are twisting and darting frenetically, in contrast to the calmness of the kids. Suddenly, the chickens erupt into a squawking frenzy. "Was it something I said?" I say, and in my dream Kim and I laugh. The children, so solemn before, break into giant smiles at our laughter. My heart melts. Those Kahlua-liquid eyes, so wide, so deep, hold unfathomable magic in them. I'm moved to an ancient maternal pride. Their cheeks are round under high cheekbones, and their skin dark as mahogany. *Mayan Indians?* I wonder.

In my dream, Kim and I stare, captivated, by their open, pure curiosity. We have a smiling contest, back and forth—white women and ancient brown children. Mama and Papa are smiling now, too. They adjust the chickens and cluck at them to stop their squawking. The chickens obey.

%% %% %%

I wake up with a start. Kim has taken the brochure out of my hands and is looking at it. "What the heck? What time is it?" I ask.

"Time for you to wake up and hear more Mayan history, listen to this." She reads, "'Chichén Itzá was founded around 550 AD by the Mayans.' That makes it about, oh, roughly one thousand, five-hundred years old. 'The name translates to 'at the mouth of the Itza well.' It says that it existed as a ceremonial center for the Mayan civilization."

My mind wanders away from Kim's reading of the brochure. I don't want to know from brochures. I want to know from touching, from experiencing. I wonder what the children and chickens in my dream mean—if there is some message there.

A few hours later when we approach the Mayan ruins, something in my mind and body shifts. Even though it is hot, the hair on my skin rises and chills follow. I see why this is one of the seven wonders of the current world. *How did they build these structures with their bare hands*? I love the symmetry of the buildings and how they placed them on the grounds. It is clear that the ancient Mayans were a people ahead of their time.

Kim reads again from the brochure as we walk along. "The brochure says that the Maya were talented mathematicians and astronomers, which was the basis for the infamous Mayan calendar that ends in December, 2012. There are remnants all over Chichén Itzá of the monuments they built to observe and commemorate the movements of the moon, the sun and Venus."

"What do you think will happen on December 21, 2012?" I ask.

"I don't know. Do you really believe 'the world' is coming to an end, like some people believe?" Kim asks.

"No, but I do believe the Mayans knew something would happen in 2012—an important shift of some sort. So, who knows, maybe some part of our world and the destructive ways we deal with it will come to an end."

"Wouldn't that be amazing and wonderful?"

℃ ℃ ℃

We don't talk anymore and Kim wanders off. I am drawn to the temple of *Kukulkan*—a Maya deity with feathers. Wow, I've seen a picture of this famous pyramid a bunch of times, but viewing it in person is thrilling. The pyramid was referred to in our brochure as El Castillo and is ninety-eight feet high. There are staircases on four sides. Another shift happens in me—a shift in time and space. I feel like I'm at the top of the

54

pyramid, although my body hasn't moved from the base. It is so weird, but a lightness fills my chest and I feel suddenly that looming concerns in my life diminish in the grandeur of design and the breadth of time I'm connecting to.

I recall vividly a time when, as a little girl, my first dog died and my dad had said, "I know you feel terrible about Mink, but in the grand scheme of things, this is just a short blink of time. Mink is fine and you'll love lots more dogs in your life."

I didn't know what "the grand scheme of things" meant at the time, but standing here now, I sure do—I'm looking at it. And my problems seem to have vanished.

I've seen spectacular architecture in many sites all over this world, but wonder why am I more emotionally connected here than anywhere else I've been? I feel as if there's an energy rooting up through my feet from the earth. I feel tied to the history as if I'd lived here. As I look at this massive, amazing building, I feel linked to everyone who walks around it: to those arriving by bus, to those leaving, to the villagers in the towns we drove through, even to the family in my dream. And then, I realize that the greatest connection seems the hardest to describe; but it has something to do with connecting to me—to my essence. That "something" has to be revived, but has been there all along. Tears brim my eyes, then salt my cheeks and evaporate.

After a long while, I find Kim, who stands by the Great Ball Court. As I spot her, she turns, and with a flutter of a wave begins strolling towards me. *Is she walking slowly because of the heat or is she a bit mesmerized too?*

ᖇ ᖇ ᖇ

On the bus ride home we talk about the strangeness of time, how sometimes it slows down, sometimes speeds up; it isn't the steady metronome we came to think it was as adults.

"I can't believe it's already been eight months since we were last here in Playa, it seems like five minutes ago. I feel as young as a child and as old as a sage at the same time." As I say this I am reminded of the children and their parents in my dream… maybe they are parts of me—even the squawking chickens!

Kim turns to me and says, "Guess what? We win!"

"Oh, yeah, we are definitely winning!"

This has become our little private joke. Since our last trip here, we decide that we are having way more fun in our lives than 'what's-his-name' is having in his life with 'what's-her-name'. So, at the end of the day, we win! This makes me feel giddy, too.

I look out the window and ruminate. I can't get Playa out of my mind. Even though I've been busy with my 'new' life: a new house, a new boyfriend, and a quest to find a new career, I feel this enormous pull toward Playa and the Yucatán Peninsula. *What's happening to me? Our trip to Chichén Itzá today gives me a clue; but what is the mystery behind this strange experience?*

I definitely have a new sensation happening. It's almost like those feelings of growth spurts I experienced in puberty—an excited energy that is both baffling and electrifying.

I need to share this feeling with Kim. "I feel like Playa is part of a new me. I belong to her and she belongs to me. I feel at home in Playa."

"Yes, you seem very drawn to this place."

"I am; do you think there is a Mayan Spell?"

"Playa is rumored to be built on sacred grounds, so maybe there is some truth to that," Kim says.

"Actually, I do feel grounded here," I say, hardly hearing Kim as I try to describe, mostly to myself, this new place I'm in. Then I say something completely unlike me. "I feel the land whispering to me of ancient secrets and the sea pounding on my heart with songs of heroes and heroines."

Kim stares at me for a long moment.

I snort. "What's gotten into me? I don't have a poetic bone in my body! I don't even like poetry."

"Well, Pal, at the moment you seem more ethereal than grounded!" Kim says, and then adds, "You're kind of like those Irish heroines, standing on the bluff overlooking the sea, the wind rustling your long skirts and wild hair, fire in your eyes, just before you save your country from imminent destruction."

"Hey, speaking of poetic! Are you and I under a spell or something?"

"Ha! I dunno. Maybe. There's no telling what might come out of our mouths or imaginations, right?"

I blurt out, "Yeah, I may even start writing that book I've been saying I'm going to write for the last ten years."

Kim snorts, "Well, make sure I'm a heroine in that book and you get a very tall, very pretty, A-list actress to play me in the movie."

I mimic her snort. Then we both laugh the free and happy laughs of lighthearted women who haven't forgotten what it's like to be girls.

Chapter 14

THE MARKS

"**K**IM, GUESS WHO IT IS?" BACK IN OUR ROOM, I'M ON THE PHONE, pacing, while my handsome caller back in Colorado is answering his call waiting.

"Let me guess, Mark #2?"

"You got it!" I put my hand over the phone and whisper. "It's kind of sweet that he misses me."

"Yeahbut (it sounds like "yabbut"), you've only been dating for three weeks," Kim says.

"Well, I followed all your love-rehab advice and voila, I am actually a goddess after all. Think it can be and it is!"

"Oh, boy!" Kim shakes her head and grins at the same time Mark #2 comes back on the line.

"Oh, hi again! Yeah, I'm still here. I'm just getting into my bikini."

He's playful and his voice is lighter than usual. "No, I don't have a camera on this phone and even if I did, I can't now; Kim's nearby." I wink at her.

Kim rolls her eyes, giving me the look, *Don't you dare have phone sex with me in this room.*

"No, it's okay, we're just hot to trot to get to the beach."

He says something about being hot and I giggle and pace some more. I know I'm teasing him a little and he's not used to it, I guess, but he seems to be enjoying it.

"Okay, now really, Kim's been waiting to go, so I gotta skedaddle. What? Oh, that must be a hold-over term from my Texas days. Anyway, thanks for calling. Sure, talk to you later. Bye, Mark."

"Question: You complain about his calling so often, so why do you pick up every time he calls?" Kim asks.

"I don't know. I guess I was raised to be a polite and courteous girl." I smile.

"Yeahbut you're just complying with his wishes. It encourages him."

"Yeahbut," I say, giggling and mocking Kim, "I think he quite likes me, and I haven't experienced that in a long, long, time."

"Yeahbut, yesterday you were calling him 'pesky.' I'm just saying…"

Hmmmm… I'm certainly getting a lot of yeahbuts!

❀ ❀ ❀

While daydreaming on the beach, I think about Marc #1 as we sometimes call my ex now that I'm dating Mark #2. I'm remembering how it was with us at the beginning.

We'd been working together for about three years. In fact, he'd recruited me out of college. Our work relationship had evolved into a friendship, especially as he was helping me through my divorce. At some point, our friendship progressed into fond and caring feelings for each other. The next step seemed obvious even though it was against company policy to date fellow workers. So, we had to be secretive. Sneaking around added to the fun, and I had butterflies for months as he played hard-to-get.

I close my eyes and go into a kind of reverie. We are in the airport in Puerto Rico with a bunch of co-workers, laughing about the correct spelling of "espresso." I thought it was spelled "expresso," and he said, "No, it's spelled 'espresso,'" and we bet twenty dollars on it. I, of course, lost the bet.

"You owe me twenty dollars. Cough it up, BAM!" he says. (He called me by my initials.)

"Can't right now, but I'll get it to you Monday," I say.

"I don't know; this is a pretty serious issue!" he says with a mocking, crooked smile.

That Monday, I go to the bank and get twenty-dollars worth of Japanese yen in small denominations; put it in an envelope and onto his desk. A few minutes later, he runs into my office on some pretext or another, closes the door and manages a serious face. "This form of payment is unacceptable. How am I to know if it equals twenty dollars?" He hands me the envelope, closes my door and nuzzles my neck. I'm very much aroused by our fun and his kisses, so agree we'll sneak out for lunch… maybe to his place.

For weeks, I brought him envelopes of different currencies: Russian rubles, Mexican pesos, British pounds. Each time he refuses the form of payment.

The day I gave him twenty-dollars worth of Danish krones, he didn't refuse them, thanked me instead and invited me to lunch. When the bill came he placed the krones, rubles, pesos and pounds in the guest check presentation holder and handed it to the waiter without missing a beat—continuing his conversation with me as if all were normal. The waiter returned, red-faced, with the manager behind.

"Uh, sorry, sir, we cannot take foreign currency."

Marc, glanced over at me, then replied "Uh, sorry, sir, but you're going to have to take that up with the lady sitting across the table from me."

The waiter looked at me. Marc could hardly keep a straight face.

Then the manager looked at me. "Oh my gosh, I apologize. Here's my card," I said as I pulled it out and slapped it down on the table. When the waiter and manager turned away, carrying my credit card, Marc exploded into laughter and I punched him in the arm. He gave me back all the foreign currency and patted my hand paternally. I was half furious at being duped, but had to laugh, seeing him laugh so hard.

Still whining that I have not paid up on my twenty-dollar bet, I devise a brilliant plan to get even with him for stiffing me with the restaurant bill. One night, I make brownies and affix a U.S. twenty-dollar bill between two paper plates that hold the brownies on top.

WHY You No Scream ViVA?!

But he refuses to eat the brownies, saying, "You probably cut up that twenty-dollar bill into tiny pieces and baked them in there. I'm not going to eat those!"

This fun, ongoing gag becomes a great source of creativity and playfulness, which seemed to delight us both.

℅ ℅ ℅

I'm jolted back to the present by the piercing sound of a lifeguard's whistle. I sit up, startled.

Kim asks, "Have a nice nap?"

"Dreamy, but I wasn't sleeping, exactly. I remembered a time with Marc #1, when we were first dating. I'd forgotten how fun he was—so playful and irreverent."

"Yeah, Marc's basically a pretty hilarious guy."

"It was so wonderful, I want that dream back."

"I hate to remind you how that dream ended… that big jerk."

"How could I forget," I say, my dream deflating fast.

I try not to remember that shocking conversation when he went from telling me, "I need some space to find myself" to finally admitting, "I have met someone else and I don't want to be with you anymore!"

"Why did you have to remind me?"

"I'm sorry, but I don't want you going backwards, Pal. Let's get to the present and talk about future possibilities. You are dating a really nice guy who you seem kind of smitten with and who, I quote, 'quite likes me', right?"

I nod, then hear the scuba diving class flip flopping in their flippers towards the edge of the pool. And I'm happy for the distraction. I'm not sure I can talk about Mark #2 so soon after that lovely memory of Marc #1.

The beginning divers are awkward under the weight of tanks and wetsuits. I can't help but smile at the earnest look on their faces as they cradle their masks and line up along one side of the pool facing the instructor who is in the water. When I look at Kim, she's peering over the rim of her sunglasses with a bemused expression. We look at each other and laugh as the beginner's class looks like gigantic penguins standing on the side of the pool.

"Last chance to learn how to scuba dive, Pal!" Kim says.

"After you, girlfriend."

"Well, as much as I'd love to, I'd rather talk about men right now, specifically *your* man. So back to the subject at hand. Is Mark #2 a good prospect?"

"Well, the difference between Marc #1 and Mark #2 is that Mark #2 gets so serious and intense sometimes. I miss playful and funny."

"Okay, so you have to weigh these things. Do you want 'serious' or 'fun?' Do you want 'open-book' or 'complicated?' Do you want a guy who is really checked-in and emotionally available or someone kind of aloof, yet alluring?"

"Yeah, all good questions. At least Mark #2 wants to be with me, but he's a little domineering and I keep wondering how I can maintain my sense of self without being consumed." "Hmmm, that is a concern, but don't you think that can be worked out by setting boundaries?"

"Probably, but I'm not very good at that. And right now, it's pretty irresistible to be pursued and desired again. I like the feeling of being lovable, of being attractive—I mean, he says he craves me and other wonderful things. There is something very sexy and mysterious about his intensity."

"Well, then maybe you just want to go with that flow and not do the boundaries thing." Kim takes a drink from her iced tea and clicks it down into the cup holder on her recliner.

"Maybe." I adjust my towel.

"Maybes are killers. They keep a person stuck in uncertainty. Gotta make some choices, then go with them."

"I know. I do love that Mark #2 is on a spiritual journey—that's exciting. Marc #1 never seemed interested in anything like that. Maybe

Mark #2 is *too* good. He doesn't seem to have an ounce of 'bad boy' in him. I'm rather fond of 'bad boys' and I miss that about Marc #1!" I take my hat off, shake out my hair, airing out the sweaty hair underneath where I'd been lying on it.

"I wouldn't worry about that. Every man I've ever met has a bad-boy side, even if they keep it under wraps. He just hasn't revealed it to you, yet!" Kim closes her book on the bookmark and changes positions.

I shift my position also, to see her better. "Yeah, maybe I don't really 'know-him-know-him,' yet."

Just then, the scuba-diving instructor yells some commands as the submerged students come to the surface and take off their masks.

Kim asks, "Do you want to? I mean, get to know Mark #2?"

"I think so, but I'm a bit scared of being rushed into a whirlwind which turns out to be a vortex."

"Hmm… I think we're back to boundaries, then."

"Isn't it a bit late?"

"Never too late. Frankly, I'm predicting lots of men and lots of boundaries in your future. What do you think?"

I sigh, exhausted from our discussion. I look at Kim's smiling, reassuring face with her funny pink and orange sunglasses pulled up on her head, and I feel better.

"We win?" I ask, still feeling a bit vulnerable and tentative. "We absolutely, positively win!" Kim says and takes another sip of iced tea. "Oh, I found another great quote in this book I'm reading that could pertain to your moving on from Marc #1. It's from C.S. Lewis and goes like this; 'Getting over a painful experience is much like crossing monkey bars. You have to let go at some point in order to move forward.'"

"I love that!" I say, and decide not to think about the Marks anymore. "Hey, let's go do something fun without boundaries!"

Kim laughs. "I've got just the ticket—finger painting over in the children's area!"

"That's about my speed today, let's go!"

The Marks

Finger painting's a hoot, no limits enforced, just splish-splashing the paint around in great swirls of color—it's liberating and silly.

Boundaries are a funny thing. You have to know when to set them and when to let them go.

Chapter 15

Diluted or Full Strength?

I T'S AROUND DUSK THE SAME DAY AND WE SWIM TO THE BAR AT THE end of the pool and order gin and tonics. Then, after floating around, we find a place to lounge to watch the sunset which should happen in about fifteen minutes. It's beginning to streak the sky with pale colors.

"Well, this is a nice tonic drink with a smidge of gin!" I say, toweling off.

"You know what they say about all-inclusives—the drinks are always watered down." Kim says, matter-of-factly. She puts on the terrycloth robe provided by the resort.

"Speaking of all-inclusives, have you noticed that everyone here, with maybe one or two exceptions, is a middle-class, white person from the States?" I ask.

"Except for the staff, yes, and those cultivating a tan trying to look Latin!"

"Ha! Yeah! Well, I'm not complaining, mind you, I mean, we have all the amenities, but I don't feel the kind of magic I felt when we were at Chichén Itzá. Didn't you feel kind of transported there?"

"If you mean a feeling of being elevated into a vast and ancient world—magical and even mystical? Yep, I did."

"Are you quoting from the tour book again?"

"Who me?" Kim giggles. "I did feel an eerie sense of infinite time going backwards and forwards."

"Me too. And I don't feel we can find that here. It's too safe, too organized and regimented," I say.

"I know what you mean. Are you feeling herded, by any chance?"

I sit up a little straighter in my terrycloth bathrobe. "Yes! That's it. Remember the scuba-divers lined up like penguins this morning? Now, *they* were being herded!"

"Yep. How 'bout the buffet line? I always feel like a sheep bunched up in lines at that eating pavilion." Kim adds.

"Me, too. And, in the organized games and activities, I feel like I'm part of a call for cows. Speaking of losing your identity..."

"I believe the term is 'cattle call' and yeah, *this isn't really us.* We are more the adventurous types and although female, we are *not* cows."

"Mooooo! Maybe you're not!"

Kim laughs because my 'moo' is quite loud and heads turn.

I continue. "I feel a little stifled here. I want more adventure and excitement. I feel like I'm in a protective cocoon here."

"In other words, you're a risk-seeker. Me too!" Kim says.

"Problem is, I feel obligated to eat, drink and play here, having spent so much money for having it all in one place. Don't you?"

"That's the trap. Next time, let's stay in Playa del Carmen—the real Mexico. Maybe we can get some of that magic back that we found at the ruins."

"Ruins. Huh, a light bulb just turned on when you said that. You know how, back home, I've been saying that Marc #1 and I... that our eleven-year relationship is in ruins?"

"I heard that once or twice!" Kim says with a trace of sarcasm.

"Well, when I had that daydream about him back there, it was as if I was floating above the ruins of our relationship and I saw the magic in it. I mean, the gift of it was magical and kind of timeless, in a way."

"Nice. That's very nice—seeing the presence of magic from above the ruins."

Strength?

We are silent a while, each in our own thoughts as the sunset bathes us in an unearthly light; a timeless and dramatic event. *The Ancient Mayans saw this same sunset*, I muse. *Over all those years of their very precise calendar. And we, we are so fortunate to feel the vastness of this universe, overlooking the Caribbean here in Mexico.*

Kim breaks the silence. "The all-inclusives might be limiting, but nature isn't, is it? Look at this magnificent display."

"Amazing. All the colors. Wow."

We absorb the beauty for a long time, then I whisper, "It's as if the sunset's telling us, 'don't settle for anything less than the whole spectrum.'"

Kim nods.

"What would life be like if we never had to settle for anything less than what we can envision and want?"

I take a deep breath and hug my knees up to my chest, then add, "I don't want to settle anymore, Kim. I mean it."

"I'm with you, Pal."

Chapter 16

THE THIRD WHEEL

K IM STARTS DATING A WONDERFUL MAN, WHOM WE CALL "QUATRO," because Kim's feeling quite sure they will marry—making him husband number four. He and his friends book a week at a hotel in Cancun (also in the Riviera Maya) not far from Playa. After Kim and I get home from Playa, I am invited to go with them to Cancun at the last minute because someone can't make it. Because the Riviera Maya is "my healing place" and seems to be a big part of my spiritual journey, I jump at the chance, even though Kim and I had been there the month before.

ॐ ॐ ॐ

I'm cheerfully going up the elevator to my room in the hotel, anxious to see my accommodations for the next week. After I enter room #2213, I notice an open piece of luggage on the second queen-size bed and realize I have a roommate. Upon entering the bathroom, I notice the counter is strewn with a razor, aftershave, and cologne. I peer into the open toiletry bag and yep, there's a package of condoms. Uh, oh.

I hurry out to the bedroom in order to dial Kim's room, and I see a bunch of Tommy Bahama shirts hanging in the open closet and piles of this mystery guy's underwear and tee-shirts sitting atop the chest of drawers. I momentarily think to myself, *Maybe*

I should see what this guy looks like before I protest my unexpected circumstances. But then I dial Kim's room.

"Hi, how's your room?" Kim asks, when I announce myself.

"You didn't tell me I'd be bunking with a guy!"

"What?" she shouts, horrified!

"Yep, there's some guy's stuff all over the room."

"Stay right there, I'm coming down. This has got to be a mistake."

When Kim gets to the room she looks around, seeing how mystery man has definitely planted himself for the duration, she motions for me to follow her. "C'mon, the hotel must have put you in this room as a substitute for the guy—the 'missing person' who couldn't make it on the trip." (That "missing person" would become an important part of my adventures later on.)

"Maybe they thought Brooke was a man. So, come on up to our suite, you can stay with us."

"Oh, I can't do that. You need your privacy. No, I'll just get a room."

"Can't. They're all sold out and besides," Kim explains, "we have a pull-out couch in our living room and our bedroom is behind closed doors. It'll be fun. Quatro likes you."

I follow her and bask in Kim's friendship and easy solution. As usual, she's light and reassuring. And the single, mystery man is funny when he finds out I'd inspected his room. "It's fine with me if we share a room; I'll be a perfect gentleman—unless you don't want me to be!"

But no, I decide to room with Kim and Quatro even if I'm clearly the third wheel. This is the first in a series of discomforts made bearable by humor. At the time, I don't think these events are part of the spiritual journey of Playa I so long to take, but I am to discover that, good or bad, they all lead to more awakenings.

There are four single guys, a lot of pot smoking and sopho-moric humor going on whenever the group was out doing things together. As I have never seen the appeal of pot, I don't indulge; but I feel a bit like a prude. I'm not pure, mind you. I've tried it plenty of times. It just doesn't do much for me, not like a good margarita or glass of wine. And so, even though Mark #2 keeps calling me (which becomes a running joke with the single guys), I am beginning to appreciate his depth of character.

The next little red flag pops up when one of the single guys in our party keeps disappearing from the group—for hours—whether we're at a local restaurant, a club or a tourist-type outing. Kim and I feel there is something "off" about the guy. He is kind of creepy and, comparing notes, several of us decide he must be out scoring drugs (which are so available down here) and getting high elsewhere with heavier stuff because our group was just too tame for him.

On the last day, Creepy Guy approaches Kim, Quatro and I at the hotel restaurant with this story. "I lost my accommodations at my hotel for tonight and need a place to stay. Can I sleep in your place?"

Kim and I hurry off to the restroom to confer. "He's shady to begin with," I say. "I wonder if he's making up the story for some reason."

"Yeah, and if it is true, what did he do to get ejected from his accommodations?"

"I do not feel comfortable with him in our space," I say.

But when we return from the restroom, Quatro has agreed to Creepy Guy's request and it is a fait accompli. Hmmm, I wonder what that means? I'll bet I have to sleep on the other queen bed in the bedroom with Kim and Quatro. Oh, that will be fun. *I am so not liking being a third wheel.*

‰ ‰ ‰

The rest of our group has red-eye flights tonight and will miss our last evening of the trip. So, it ends up being just the four roomies—Kim,

Quatro, Creepy Guy and me—hanging out together... *Hmmm... now how did that happen?* At dinner, Creepy Guy does an about-face and is suddenly charming and cute and quite entertaining. I'm skeptical, watchful, because I think he might be working me for a little booty. And believe me, I do not find that idea appealing at all. Besides I am dating Mark #2.

After dinner, we decide to walk along the boulevard on the Bay side. It's a serene night, with balmy breezes, a vast sprinkling of stars and fragrances of tropical flowers sweetening the air. It's a perfect, romantic night and of all the people in the world, I am stuck with Creepy Guy. And on top of that, he asks me, "May I hold your hand?"

I feel like I'm in sixth grade again, shrug and say, "Um, okay." I immediately start justifying this decision to myself, *It's just easier to say yes than embarrass or reject a guy on a harmless request like this. But why the hell did I just agree to that? I'm so not interested in him. But what am I going to say, "No, I don't want to hold your grubby little hand?" What if he takes it the wrong way, though, and thinks I'm interested in hooking up later. Sometimes, I don't like how easily I comply with men's wishes.*

"Oh, look," Quatro says. "There's a guy with a parrot and a camera. Let's go get our picture taken."

When it is my turn to have the parrot perch on my shoulder, the photographer says, a few seconds too late, "Oh wait, I need you to take off your glasses." But that parrot is quick. He's already chomping down on my glasses. Everyone laughs and I hold them while I paste on a smile for the picture. I'm still uncomfortably anxious about Creepy Guy wanting to hold my hand and what he's thinking my agreement to that means.

After our cozy little group gets back to our suite, Creepy Guy asks me to watch a movie with him.

"No, thanks," I huff a laugh, "I'm going to bed and I am going to lock the door behind me!" *Ha! I think to myself. See, I'm not such a pushover after all.*

And so we three do, we lock the door and go to bed. In the dark; Kim, her boyfriend and I all get the giggles about being in the same sleeping room together. We laugh about all the funny, quirky events of the past days.

Quatro laughs, "I will never forget you singing country songs at the top of your lungs two nights ago in the hot tub. Who knew you were such a diva! And you drew a crowd."

Kim joined him, "I loved how total strangers joined in; and the more they did, the more you owned the place, spreading your arms wide and embracing the whole resort! It was so fun… and funny."

Sometimes I shock myself. "Yeah, who knew I had that in me." I'm warmed by the thought and get comfortable under the light blanket.

Recalling *The Waltons,* I say, in a sing-song voice, "Well, Night, Quatro-Boy!"

Catching on, Quatro says, in an equally sappy voice, "Goodnight, Brookie-Girl!"

Kim chimes in with a smile in her voice, "Goodnight, Brookie, goodnight Quatro-ie!"

I add in a whisper, "Goodnight, Creepy Guy! Sleep well on the other side of this locked door!"

And we all get the giggles.

ળ ળ ળ

In the morning, Creepy Guy has disappeared. I pick up my glasses from the table and see a whopping chunk of plastic chipped out of the temple. They are ruined and I immediately wonder if Creepy Guy exacted revenge upon me for rebuffing his charming ways. I cannot fathom what he could possibly have done to ruin my eyeglass frames like this. My mind is racing. And then, paranoia sets in, we all begin to look in our wallets and luggage in the living room. Perhaps he's a thief to support his drug habit. His whole story about losing his accommodations on the last day was kind of fishy.

But nothing's missing. And we see him at breakfast; clean and cheerful, drinking coffee and munching on tropical fruit. Embarrassed, I remember it was dark when the parrot ate my glasses and I never put them back on, and I might have been a bit tipsy. In my mind I falsely accused him. Not okay but a bit beside the point. The point is, there's something not feeling right around here, but what?

❧ ❧ ❧

I PONDER THIS ON THE PLANE RIDE HOME. PLANE TRIPS ARE SO GOOD for sorting things out, right? What did I like about this trip, didn't like? I liked being with Kim and Quatro and the beauty of the Yucatán always revives me, but I didn't like being a tag-along. I have to admit, when Kim and I first came to The Mayan Riviera, I needed someone to lean on, to pull me along. She will always be my northern star. But for now, I need to move forward on my own, find a new path, one that challenges me in a different way. I'm searching for something and even though I don't know what it is, I'm excited about it and want to go solo for a while. Where and how? I don't know, but I'll know it when I see it!

Chapter 17

PABLO'S PARADISE

IN LOOKING FOR A NEW PATH, I FEEL THAT TEACHING YOGA MAY BE a good place to start exploring. After all, yoga promises a means to inner wisdom and enlightenment. In my own yoga practice, I feel great; physically, emotionally and spiritually, and I think it would be wonderful to be able to facilitate those benefits for others. So, after getting back from Cancun, in September, I immediately enroll in a two-month, yoga-teacher certification program in Denver. In that course, ironically, is a very pretty Latina from Playa del Carmen! She has the same dark, liquid, Latin eyes and sun-kissed skin as Lalo. She also has dark brown, naturally wavy, shoulder length hair and eyelashes as long as my golden retriever's. I've always thought women with dark, Caribbean features were so exotic and beautiful. She seems kind of timid, at first, so I approach her. We chitchat about how much we both love her home town and discuss how we must meet in Playa when we are both there again.

In the middle of that program a flyer on the bulletin board of the yoga studio—announcing a yoga retreat—catches my attention. My heart leaps out of my chest. It's planned for early November, the week after my certification program concludes, on the Mayan Riviera, in the town of Tulum! Without a second's hesitation, I sign up, chuckling at how the twins, serendipity and synchronicity, have become my good companions.

❧ ❧ ❧

Amansala Eco-Chic Resort and Spa is located less than two hours south of where we were in Cancun and less than an hour south of Playa. What a difference from the other resorts I've stayed in. It is anti-tourist, anti-commercialistic—and they call it "rustic chic."

The grand, main buildings of this property are commanding and awe-inspiring! The second I walk into those buildings, I am transported, as if to another time. I feel the blood racing in my body; don't know quite why yet. After checking in at the main office, I get a tour of the massive dining room, living room and kitchen. There are some sleeping quarters in the main building and upstairs there is an area where you can hang out or do yoga. Next to the main house I explore two smaller buildings—one housing an expansive open-air yoga room, the other accommodating sleeping quarters. There's another large building further away and twenty-four cabañas on the beach. Little Tibetan flags and other fabrics flutter in the breeze; the air is soft and gentle. It is a place, I'd been told, where like-minded people come to practice yoga and connect to something bigger than the same old fun-in-the-sun tourism-type activities.

Wow, can paradise get any better than this? It is so private and quiet, I think, as we are shown to our rooms overlooking the whitest, most pristine beach I've ever seen. I have a roommate in a cabaña near the beach–a *female* roommate this time. LOL. We eat healthy, organic food, family-style around one large table. We practice yoga overlooking the Caribbean in front of the jungle, with its multi-colored-green splendor. The air seems nourished by generous amounts of negative ions from the sea water and from the CO_2 wafting over to us from lush jungle plants. This is a good thing, because yoga requires deep breathing as a first priority. Come to think of it, the word *amansala* from the Sanskrit, means "peace and water." They got that right.

The vibe here is different from other places I've been to in the Mayan Riviera—it's kind of like the difference between rock music and Mozart—here, there's a finer, lighter wavelength. This atmosphere, at first, seems to be less one of partying—where there's a focus on body sensation and "escaping from"—and more an orientation of spiritual exploration, using the breath and body to "move towards" something beyond the material world. I don't judge either one as better than the other, but this orientation is perfect for me now!

In ironic contrast to all this serenity and the atmosphere of spiritual searching, is the alleged story that this resort was once the home of Pablo Escobar, the most notorious cocaine trafficker and drug lord of Columbia and perhaps of the world. Apparently, a decade before he was gunned down near one of his nineteen homes in Columbia in 1993, he had acquired this property in Tulum and built two huge stucco mansions on it and several smaller buildings. It is rumored that he and his lieutenants and perhaps starlets from the *telenovelas*, hid away here in this secluded part of the Caribbean. Certainly, the main buildings with their thick, bullet-proof walls, the lookouts on the roof and the underground tunnel from the main building to the other tremendous villa some distance away, all bespeak cautionary measures of one who is hiding from the law!

Of course, it has all been transformed, renovated and added to by its new owner, and the whole property was allegedly "spiritually cleansed" by a Tibetan monk brought in to rid the atmosphere of any lingering, nasty vibes. Notwithstanding, there is a mischievous, daring excitement that remains—or maybe it's just my vivid imagination!

While Amansala invites spiritual awareness and expansion, it is not as if sensual or sexual pursuits are not present. (Escobar's influence perhaps?) As it is a co-educational group, some of the men and women couple up; but hooking up does not interest me at the moment. I am still dating Mark #2 back home, and my focus here is more inward: to observe and reflect as I engage in my practice. Whereas with my prior visits to Playa, I too was focusing on body sensation and "escaping from;" I am now more fully observing and attending to things with a decidedly spiritual agenda. I am and have been opening to new ideas, people and experiences and opening to more space within and without.

ॐ ॐ ॐ

There's "candlelight only" here at Amansala at night, which comforts the soul and helps with looking inward in a good way. Everything seems slowed down here, which relaxes the body and allows for deeper breathing.

The safety and security of my corporate job is now gone, but on the Riviera Maya, for some reason, I feel really safe. The angst and pain over my break-up with Marc #1 is diminishing and I'm beginning to fall in love with aspects of myself I hadn't fully seen or acknowledged before—my ability to move away from the past, to make decisions and to be someone apart from my past affiliations and identities. Or, at least I am making progress towards that. I am now forty years old, a milestone I used to think of as ancient; but here, I am experiencing again that feeling of being ageless. So I am someone apart from not only past affiliations and identities but also from aging! This realization pleasantly surprises me. Now I have to figure out a way to make this last after I leave here.

The next morning during our yoga session, I am holding a difficult pose and contemplating how to make this feeling of agelessness last forever, when a mosquito lands on my leg and starts chowing down on me. I keep my composure, though I am dying to kill *his* feeling of agelessness. *That's got to be the biggest, beefiest mosquito I have ever seen. I really must focus on my yoga pose. But I hate mosquitos. What if he's carrying the West Nile virus? I should really swat him. No—I am going to test myself and hold the pose until he flies away!* It's a small victory, but I do it! My desire to build my inner resolve is stronger than my desire to swat at that little annoyance on my leg.

Later, in the second yoga class of the day, as I'm contemplating agelessness, mosquitos, careers and world hunger, I suddenly have an epiphany; *I want to live here! I want to buy a home somewhere in the Riviera Maya. It's my soul place! That's how I can make all these empowering feelings last!*

At the end of the yoga session, I go for a little run on the beach and confirm my desire to live near the magic of Playa. When I return to Amansala, I make a call to a real estate office.

"*Bueno*, I want to look at property to buy in Playa del Carmen."

Chapter 18

BATMAN RETURNS

THE REAL ESTATE AGENT PICKS ME UP IN TULUM THE LAST DAY OF the yoga retreat. It was a gorgeous day in November and he had a small American Flag fluttering from his antenna.

He has both a big presence and big-shot name, "Hi, my name is Bruce Wayne."

"No way. C'mon, what's your real name?"

"That *is* my real name. Well, actually, my real name is Bruce Wayne Mitchell; but, when I realized how popular the superhero, Batman, is down here in Mexico, I opted to drop my surname to stand out!"

I laugh. "Okay, Batman, find me the condo of my dreams in Playa, okay? I only have a few hours before returning to the States."

After looking at several condos that underwhelm me, Batman shows me a condo I quite like, and it is listed for only one-hundred thirty-seven thousand dollars. Sweet! I think this just might be my next home—vacation home that is. He wants a down payment, but I tell him no. "I need to educate myself about purchasing in Mexico and crunch the numbers." (Yes, I am a geeky numbers person.) He looks like a dog whose bone has been confiscated. There's a pushy edge to him, more than the standard "I want to make a sale off of you" real estate agent's pushiness, and it's annoying the hell out of me.

"Don't worry, Batman, I'll be back with my expert real estate agent, Kim, who is also a designer in Colorado. That is, if I can get her to fit me into her busy schedule."

"The thing is, this condo might not be available when you return."

"Well, being Batman and all, I'm sure you can go back to your Bat Cave and find me something even more wonderful if this one's sold."

Batman shakes my hand and lingers a bit with the handshake, then walks away. Something about Batman makes me uneasy and I can't put my finger on it, but I let it go because I'm so excited about finding my dream house in Mexico.

PART THREE
Taking New Risks – Getting Out of My Comfort Zone

❀ ❀ ❀

Happiness comes from the capacity to feel
deeply, to enjoy simply, to think freely,
to risk life, and to be needed.

~ Storm Jameson ~

Chapter 19

DIRECTIONLESS IN DENVER

AFTER RETURNING HOME FROM THE YOGA RETREAT, OF COURSE, the first person I call is my multi-talented friend who affectionately calls me "Pal."

"Hi, Kim. Wanna go to Playa with me after the holidays? I need a second opinion on a condo I want to buy there."

"What?" she shrieks over the phone. "You're kidding me, right? You went to stretch your spine, not your pocketbook!"

"I am soooo not kidding. I am thrilled beyond words at the prospect of having a vacation home there. I've always wanted a beach home and that was something Marc #1 refused me."

"Wait. Okay. Wait. Brooke. Of course I want to go. Of course I'll help you, but catch me up, Pal. Sheez, I'm out of breath."

After I tell her that I need her real estate expertise and also her design acumen, she finally realizes that the rag doll who had gone with her the year before, has indeed grown a spine and some independence. She expresses her admiration and perhaps a bit of relief.

"You've come a long way, baby," she says.

"Yes, I have become a long baby this way," I return, mixing up my words on purpose this time, making her laugh. "But from now until we leave in January, I've got some more exploring to do." And I explain my plans to continue investigating a new profession. "I realized while I was on my yoga retreat that I'd rather be a yoga student than a yoga teacher.

WHY YOU NO SCREAM VIVA?!

And while I so admire yoga teachers, I'm just not sure I could support myself well enough doing that."

"Well, you're getting your teacher certificate so you'll have it if you ever want to combine it with something else."

"True. But I need to continue to explore new horizons in my work life along with the new horizons I am exploring in my personal life. I mean, don't you think it's a sign—that my job and company moved to North Carolina? I think it's the Universe giving me a nudge to break out of my corporate shell and explore other vocations that have always appealed to me. I mean, I've worked in corporate America for most of my adult life. Surely there must be something more meaningful I can contribute to the world?"

"Hey, wait, I'm remembering something. Last year, didn't you show me an astrology reading you had done that said something like you hate being a cog in a wheel and..."

"Oh my gosh, yes! I'd forgotten about that. Yeah, it said I was extremely uncomfortable in impersonal environments! That's funny, but it's not that so much. I can make my work personal, but I just want to see what's out there. And also what's in me to put out there!"

"That's adventurous. So, where are you going to start?"

"Don't laugh, but I want to explore managing animal hospitals or perhaps flipping houses."

Kim pauses and then she snorts, "I know! You could teach yoga to dogs in animal hospitals!"

"Ha ha. Very funny. You missed your calling as a career counselor!"

"Yep, that's me—right? All kidding aside, good luck with all that. Keep me posted."

℀ ℀ ℀

So I set off to explore the field of business management of veterinary hospitals. I have always adored animals and I think it would be the perfect marriage of my business experience and passion for animals.

I look into courses that would give me a flavor for this career opportunity and find a weeklong course in Denver that fits the bill. After finishing this course I realize that, while I'd enjoy the work and would be good at it, as an employee I would not be paid well enough to maintain my lifestyle. And there is a fair amount of risk and responsibility with that job. I also realize there's a high barrier to entering that profession as a consultant because I don't have the exact experience and there are several local, well-established, well-known consultants who do have years of experience in this area. I can't compete with them. Or at least it would be a long uphill battle that I don't want to undertake. So, while this profession isn't a good career path for me, I'm grateful that I've had the time and wherewithal to explore it.

I have been intrigued with the field of flipping houses, inspired by watching the television show *Flip This House*. I love the creativity of turning an old, run-down house into a lovely home that somebody will appreciate. I also love the sense of fulfillment that comes from seeing your efforts manifest into something tangible. It's hard to get that sense of fulfillment in the corporate world—at least in the area I worked in. I might get a "well done" on an earnings call script I wrote or "great work" for a PowerPoint presentation I put together. Somehow, it's just not the same as a young family saying, "Thank you for helping us get into our dream home that we can actually afford," and being able to drive by the fruits of your labor every day and see the beauty you contributed to this world.

So, the rest of November and into December, I explore this field, finding out everything I can about the business of flipping houses. I research, put together a business model, talk to lots of people in the business and watch as many episodes of *Flip This House* as I can get my hands on. But in the end, without having any real experience or education in this field, I feel it is too risky of a venture. And having built a few houses of my own and knowing the headaches and logistical nightmares it can wreak when subcontractors don't show up or do the work properly, I decide that there are too many un-controllables.

Damn. I'm back to square one. At this point, feeling the need for answers, I think about looking at that old horoscope. I dig it out, read it over and something catches my eye. It says, "Your sense of wonder and your openness to the unseen, subtle, spiritual dimensions of life are two of your gifts. You are extremely sensitive to the energies and currents of feeling around you and, Brooke, you are so impressionable and receptive, you are influenced (even duped) rather easily."

I ponder this carefully. Duped, eh? Maybe I'm duped by astrology! LOL. I mean, just because I was born at a certain time, in a certain place… I mean, does every person born in the same city as me at the same time have the same horoscope? And why am I looking for answers outside of myself anyway? In the end, I decide that it's like anything else outside of you: something you read in a book, see in a movie, or something someone tells you about yourself, if it resonates deeply within yourself, then those outside things are only reflecting what you already know in your heart. I know I have the capacity for wonder and I am sensitive to and interested in things you can't really see. The strange thing is, I have an experience that very day that reminds me of a deep interest and leads me to my next career subject to explore. Perhaps it was just the increased awareness brought by re-reading the horoscope that opened my eyes to a new opportunity?

I am playing with my beautiful golden retrievers and notice one is a bit down in the mouth. She's restless, whining in a way I don't understand and looking at me through miserable eyes. I feel frustrated at not being able to find out why she's so uncharacteristically unhappy. I try all the usual things; feeding her, taking her for a walk, but she continues to mope and whine. I'm a very concerned mom at this point, but a trip to the vet tells me nothing obvious is wrong with her and that it must be something "other than physical."

Great. Now what? It is then I remember my good friend, Cindy, an expert in animal communication. So, I call her up. She asks me some questions, then does something in the quiet of a minute or two. After this, I look at my disturbed doggy, and she gives a big yawn and settles down immediately, head on paws, tail wagging. I am amazed at the transformation and fire off a dozen questions over the phone—shotgun style. Cindy suggests I come out to California and take her animal communication course. I say I'd think about it.

I thank her and get off the phone. Wait, did I almost say yes to a course in animal communication? I mean, it is one thing for Cindy to communicate with animals; but me? I'm a type-A, Southern Baptist-raised, practical, I-gotta-see-it-to-believe-it kind of girl. And yet, Cindy clearly did something real and extraordinary. My snoring, calm doggy is proof!

I think about what I'd read earlier in the day on my horoscope and get chills. I've clearly been on a path this past year to discover and develop my telepathy or intuition or extra sensory perception—or whatever it is! And so, I rally my moxie and fly to California to Cindy's wonderful home high up in the mountains to investigate another career path and perhaps learn a new skill I can use with my four-legged children. I mean, *¿por qué no?*

Chapter 20

TELEPATHY, REALLY?

CINDY HAS BEEN A VETERINARY TECHNICIAN AND A PROFESSIONAL animal communicator for over twenty years and has communicated with animals her entire life. I take her two-day workshop, during which she teaches me the techniques to communicate telepathically with animals. Then we practice on her animals: six cats, four birds, three horses, two dogs and one bunny! I am surprised to discover that there's a technique to this endeavor. I thought you would just start talking to animals and they would talk back! But there is a true technique that can be taught and learned. Although nothing is as effective as taking the workshop in person with Cindy, I will summarize as best I can.

First you get centered and ground yourself. I learn about chakras so that I can learn to open my heart chakra. (Chakras, according to Wikipedia: "In Hindu metaphysical tradition and other belief systems, are centers of Prāna, life force, or vital energy. Chakras correspond to vital points in the physical body.") I practice this and feel a bit of a shift, maybe. Then, I am instructed in how to go through a list of prescribed questions to ask telepathically. I am forewarned that telepathic communication doesn't always look like our normal channels of communication. Cindy advises, "Sometimes they give you a word or concept, and sometimes they give you a picture. Accept whatever they give you and then move on to the next question. When you are done with your list of questions, thank them for being open to talking to you and bid them farewell."

After I practice with about eight of her animals, asking approximately ten questions each, we stop and debrief for the day. She helps me interpret the answers. She says that I'm doing well—getting the right answers about sixty percent of the time—a great start.

On the second day of her two-day course, I have an experience with her bunny, Sammy, that turns me into a believer.

I am sitting with the bunny and centering myself; using yoga breath and opening my heart chakra through visualization. I ask the bunny, telepathically, Sammy, what is your favorite room in this house?

Sammy sends me a picture of a beautiful butterfly. Or, maybe it is me making this picture up? It really isn't an answer to the question, but Cindy has instructed me to fully accept whatever answer is given even if it doesn't make sense. I thank Sammy for his answer and go on to more questions.

When I debrief with Cindy, she pauses and says, "Well, Sammy spends all his time in my office where I have a lot of angel figurines, so maybe in his bunny mind he thinks anything with wings is a butterfly." I think, *Okay, that's a stretch, but okay.* Later that day we go to her office for something (I had not been in her office prior to that) and right when I walk into her office, on the wall in front of me, is a picture of a butterfly. I stand there for a full five seconds with my jaw on the ground and goose bumps all over and say, "Cindy, do you see what I see?"

Cindy looks where I'm staring and grins, looking very pleased. "I'd forgotten all about that picture. Well done, very well done getting his answer."

I had a marvelous, consciousness-expanding time with Cindy and feel exhilarated that I've explored something that had always caught my curiosity. I don't obtain a new profession out of the work with Cindy, but I not only acquire an open mind to controversial ideas but also gain a lifelong ability for communicating better with animals. *Ha!* I thought to myself, *maybe I can even try this with two-legged, male animals!*

Chapter 21

It's You, Not Me

Mark #2 and I have been dating since July—about six months. In the area of male-female relationships, I am becoming more and more depressed and enter my "winter blues." I think maybe it starts with the one-year anniversary of the break-up with Marc #1 in October, but in any case I need to resolve this mounting tension and increasing weariness. As December progresses, I become increasingly unsure of things, and I'm not myself. I can't figure it out exactly; I am feeling pushed around by Mark #2's emotions and unable to articulate my own. *Have I been subsumed into a man's dominion again, somehow subservient to his needs? Grrrrr.*

An attorney by training, he is strong-willed and hard-headed. But the activities of the last few months have made me stronger willed. I have less and less self-doubt, except when it comes to Mark #2. I'm still a bit indecisive around him and I feel smothered. I know I am as strong as he, deep down; but something is off with me, with us.

As the holidays approach, I hibernate at home and don't go out with friends, and this scares the hell out of me as I am reminded of the two months that I hibernated at home after the break-up with Marc #1. I never want to feel that low again.

❧ ❧ ❧

Two things happen with Mark #2 during the month of December. He tells me he's going on a family trip with his children, parents and his ex-wife, and he doesn't invite me. The second incident involves again being excluded from his son's family birthday party. I'm developing big reservations about him and his commitment to me, to us.

%% %% %%

I am heading to Texas to visit my family for Christmas, and he comes to spend the night with me on the eve before I depart. We go out for dinner and there is awkwardness between us. I am feeling very uneasy tonight, especially after we get home.

"Let's go to bed, Brooke."

"Not yet for me, you go on up. I have to go into my office to book my trip to Playa with Kim."

"You know, it irks me that you haven't invited me to any of your trips to Mexico. I feel really left out and that hurts, frankly."

Interesting he feels left out, what about his excluding me from his family outings?

"I'm sorry your feelings are hurt. But this is something Kim and I do together—and this is just a quick trip with a specific mission. Make yourself comfortable, I'll be there in a few."

With a big huff, he turns to go upstairs.

The tension is so heavy it is hard for me to breathe. *Did I say, 'make yourself comfortable?' Ha! Hardly seems possible for either of us tonight.* It is then I remember my work with Cindy. I get centered and try to quiet myself, wondering what he is going through. *What are you feeling, Mark, that you're not saying?* I ask, telepathically.

A few of words enter my mind: *frustration, loneliness, disconnection,* just like when I practiced at Cindy's.

And it keeps coming. *You are not being the person I want.*

And then a shift happens and it hits me, *Are you the person I want?*

I finish booking my trip, and on the way upstairs, even though a feeling of dread seizes up my belly, I seem to be super in touch with my own intuition. I go into my bedroom and sit on the edge of the bed. The room is dark and I can't tell at first if he's asleep.

"Are you awake?"

"Completely."

"I am going to be direct with you, Mark. I need some space, some time away from you."

We're both startled by what I blurt out. He sits up, turns on the light and peers at me, frowning. I sit very still with hunched shoulders and my throat tight—very uncomfortable. Finally, he shakes his head and combs his hands through his hair. I want to put a hand on his knee, to reassure him. *But of what? I can't reassure him about anything.* So I refrain. I have to say something. I want to say, "I'm pretty sure you feel I'm not being the woman you want and I need some space to decide what I want." But I'm chicken, so instead I say, "I'm going to Texas tomorrow to see my parents for Christmas, and I would like to take that time to sort my feelings out."

"Alright, if you say so." He gets up, puts on his clothes and walks downstairs and out my front door. I don't move, but stare at where his head had made an indentation in the pillow. I wait until I hear him start up his little Miata, then go downstairs to lock the door. I look out my living room window, my forehead against the cold pane and watch as it starts to snow. I feel I've done something brave even though my whole body is trembling at the thought that in saying something that brings him displeasure, I may lose him completely.

Overnight, the snow turns into a massive blizzard—a "storm of the century" and they close the Denver airport so I cannot go to Texas. I am stranded in my own house, eating nothing but soup mixes for the foreseeable future because I, of course, cleaned out my refrigerator in anticipation of going out of town. Had Mark #2 not left last night, we would have been trapped together in my house for three days! And his Miata would have been totally dug in. I am glad I dodged that bullet.

Mark #2 does not do well with my hiatus. He calls and leaves frustrated messages. "What do you need space for? I don't get it. Call back."

The messages become more exasperated, "Look, why don't you just break up with me if you need so much space? Call back."

Finally I call him up. He is steamed and sounds weary. I'm weary too; the depression is like an anchor pulling me under water.

"Okay, Mark," I take a deep breath. "I keep getting this feeling that I'm not being the person you want—and you are not being the person I want either. I believe we have to be the people we are, true to ourselves first, right?"

He doesn't want to hear me, and repeats his suggestion with considerable determination. "Look, if you are so unhappy with me, why don't you just break up with me."

He's worn me down. I can't take it anymore. "Okay, fine! I agree with you; let's break up." He hangs up.

I call my trusty friend Kim to break the news to her. "Well, guess what?"

"What?" she asks.

"Mark #2 is toast."

"Whaaat?"

"Yeah, I know."

"What happened?"

"I told him I needed some space and he kind of flipped out on me. He said that I should just break up with him, if I didn't know what I wanted. So I did."

"Why he no scream *viva*?"

I chuckle a bit at Kim's attempt at humor.

"Seriously, though, why was he being so unreasonable?" Kim asks.

"I think Mark is frustrated that I won't communicate my feelings to him. But how can I when I don't even know what they are? You know I've been feeling kind of depressed lately. I'm not sure if it's related to Marc #1 or Mark #2. I just wanted some space to sort it all out."

"Well, I'm not surprised. You shut your feelings down a long time ago to not feel the void with Marc #1. Feelings are like a muscle; if you don't use them, they will atrophy. You have to retrain them."

"Interesting perspective. Thanks."
"Yup. Well, hang in there, Pal."

৩ ৩ ৩

The next day I wake up, feeling oddly refreshed. My depression has totally lifted. I feel relieved and also hope beyond all hope that Mark #2 is relieved as well. It's remarkable—miraculous even, and totally unexpected. Feeling as light and bright as the new crystal flakes sparkling on top of the heaps of snow, I dream of Playa and my next trip there. I am so ready for the next leap of faith.

Chapter 22

Go Big or Go Home

I T'S JUST OVER A YEAR SINCE THE FIRST TIME I LAID EYES ON PLAYA del Carmen. Kim, now more of a sister than a caretaker, is my roommate at the *Acanto* Boutique Hotel in the center of Playa del Carmen. We'd long since graduated from all-inclusives and I am no longer her "project" or tag-along. I've asked her along, not only because we're close friends; but also because I value Kim for her expertise as a real estate agent and designer. I know no one as talented and capable. I want to know if the condo of my choice is rentable and whether or not I'll be able to resell it should I want to do so. And of course, I want to know all about the Mexican laws concerning the purchase and ownership of real estate by a foreigner.

❧ ❧ ❧

Batman meets us at his office and immediately pays all his attention to Kim. He invites us to lunch and not once does he make eye contact, let alone direct any of his information to me, the buyer. He is nice and respectful and attentive to Kim and practically ignores me the whole time. I feel like saying, *Look, asshole, I'm the one spending the money here.* It is increasingly offensive. In a meager attempt to interject my presence, I say "The salsa is the best I've ever tasted," which is true; but he ignores me. *Am I wearing man repellent, is he falling for Kim or is he simply being rude?*

When the server comes over, finally, Batman says, "Well, *finally!* We've been waiting."

"Sorry, *señor*. How can I help you?"

"By taking our orders and getting our food. We have things to do."

"*Si, señor,*" the waiter says, moving from one leg to the other, looking uncomfortable.

I feel embarrassed for Batman and on behalf of all of us "gringos."

Kim and I are not that hungry so we order one plate to split and ask for an extra plate. That request is lost in translation and they bring us an entire duplicate plate of food. We all laugh and that breaks the tension a bit, even though when the check comes, Batman scowls at the server and gives him no tip. After Kim and Batman start out the door I run back and give our server a nice tip and say I'm sorry. The waiter has a big smile for me and shakes his head in a way that tells me he isn't taking anything personally.

Over the course of dealing with Batman from that day forward, I notice how he treats Mexicans as if they are lesser persons, no matter where we go. Because he's even voiced these attitudes, I'm actually thinking of hiring a new real estate agent, but Kim says he seems to know his stuff so why not give him a chance to show us the properties? I trust Kim so, put a lid on my distaste.

Kim, not impressed with the condo I'd fallen in love with in November, tells me later that she doesn't think it meets my standards. To Batman, she simply says, "What else can you show us?"

Batman shows us higher-end condos out of my price range, so I ask him to show me ones I can afford. We look at a three-bedroom, loft-style condo in my price range, but I am under-whelmed.

Perhaps he sees that I'm feeling deflated, because he says, "While we are here, you want to see the penthouse, just for fun?"

We walk in and my heart starts racing. It is gorgeous! Now my juices are really flowing. I want it! And the hamsters on the wheel in my brain start running. I have to figure out a way to buy this penthouse. Batman says, "Well, if you think you might like this one, let me show you another penthouse in this same price range. It's in a better part of town and closer to the ocean."

This penthouse is a half block from the ocean and still under construction when we walk in. The space, the view and the ambience take my breath away. Butterflies invade my entire middle. Kim and I look at each other, eyes alight with daring and dreams. I am captivated. "Give me a day to work out the finances," I say, still holding my breath. "It is more than twice what I want to spend, but this *is* the vacation home of my dreams."

Batman smiles at me, finally.

On my own, I spend the second to last day of our four-day trip, working with my banker to figure out a way to pull this off. All my financial training kicks in and I think creatively. I ask the right questions and the answers are favorable to my being able to purchase the condominium of my dreams. Figuring this out on my own gives me a boost of self-confidence. I realize that I am competent to do things that I might have relied on Marc #1 to do previously. I feel smarter, more independent and just damn proud of myself.

On the last day of the trip, I give Batman my deposit and thank him for pushing me out of my comfort zone and for being a super hero!

Declaring it a tradition, Kim and I go to The Tequila Barrel for a drink followed by La Parilla for dinner to celebrate. This time we leave no articles of clothing behind for the gallery wall!

❦ ❦ ❦

Months later, I find out from a third party who knows Batman that he got into a fight with some locals who beat him up and he had to go back to the states to get medical treatment and to mend. First, how do I know if this story is true? I don't know for sure and I certainly hope not. But if true, why did such a thing happen to him? Had he provoked that violence with his attitudes? He once said that he didn't need to learn Spanish and that the Mexicans should learn English. My guess is that someone didn't take well to his treatment of locals and beat him up.

෯ ෯ ෯

When I see him after the alleged beating, limping and still mending, he tells me he'd fallen at a construction site. So, I don't know what is true. We can only know the truth as we experience it and I experience Batman as a competent real estate agent. But as a person, he makes me uneasy and I so protest his treating Mexicans in a condescending manner. Why would anyone do that? Prejudice. Uninspected assumptions. I do not think Americans are a superior species, entitled to special treatment, no matter their status or amount of money in their bank accounts. I'm beginning to see that living in Playa is not going to free me from the responsibility for dealing with human frailties. (Of course that will, it turns out, include my own!)

෯ ෯ ෯

When I'd seen this "superior," entitled behavior in others before, they were always covering up insecurities and self-doubts with a kind of synthetic personality of some sort. Maybe Batman is too.

I ask myself, *do I do that, even part of the time? People say that I'm genuine and forthcoming. But am I always?*

By now, I know Playa and the Riviera Maya is the magical space in which I am learning I have choices—that it is up to me to make those choices with my eyes wide open and with willingness to see and to take the consequences.

And so, Playa is also a place for me to rejuvenate and regenerate my soul. It is a place where I can expand my view of both self and the world I live in. And overall, I have Batman to thank for showing me my dream place. For that, I feel deeply grateful.

Chapter 23

CASH MULE

JUNE HAS FINALLY ARRIVED AND THE WORK ON MY CONDO IS COM-
plete! When Kim and I walk into the condo so I can take possession,
it feels like home immediately. *I've always wanted a vacation home on
the beach in Mexico and I made it happen. Not Marc #1, not Mark #2.
Just me, with a little help from my friends.* My heart fills with pride and
warmth. My dream house shimmers in exhilarating light, space, ocean
air and flowery fragrance. Giddiness mixes with a nervy-scary feeling
knowing that in a few minutes I will be handing over a big chunk of
change!

My *guapo* (handsome) builder is young, in his early thirties, but all
business. His English is fairly good and it is from him I will receive the
key. Kim is excited too, and happy to be back in Playa, eager to move
through the "taking possession procedures," which consist of looking
around to see if anything needs to be corrected or added; in other words,
developing a "punch list." Kim has lived in Asia, where, as a wife of a
VIP sales executive, she entertained hundreds of people. She has oodles
of people skills; as hostess, diplomat, real estate agent and designer. I'm
lucky to have her here making the two and a half hours' inspection that
it takes to develop a punch list. Meanwhile, I go through all the papers
that need to be signed to take possession and, of course, make the final
payment.

Everything takes a long time. In Mexico, *nothing* can be done quickly.
"*Mañana, Mañana*" is a common chant of the Mexican lifestyle. One

thinks it means "tomorrow" but it really means "not now, and I don't want to commit to when."

Finally, our duties done, Guapo hands me the key and I am as fluttery inside as a hummingbird. We shake hands and I can finally say to myself, *esta es mi casa!* (this is my house!) When they all leave, Kim and I sit and sigh for a while! I think we exchange a few dozen "wows" and then, noticing we have not said a word, start planning out all the things we have to do and rapidly go into "task mode."

The giddiness will linger for days as we figure out logistics for hunting, buying and delivering furniture and furnishings—all by pounding the pavement on foot.

We buy most of my stuff at an Indonesian store with a French name, L'Autre du Monde. This store gives one a great taste of the international flavor that abounds in Playa. Our lovely sales girl speaks with a heavy British accent and is so helpful. She even accompanies all the deliveries herself.

I have arrived in Playa with twenty-thousand dollars in travelers' checks, in denominations of one-hundred dollars each. It turns out that travelers' checks are a very outdated method of dealing with money abroad and a freakin' pain in the ass. It took two hours to sign each one of the two-hundred checks at my bank before I left Denver.

At L'Autre du Monde, my purchases total about thirteen-thousand dollars. I proudly whip out my travelers' checks and the British saleslady frowns. "I'm sorry, but we don't take travelers' checks," she says.

Then, I frown. *So, what to do?* Kim and I look at each other simultaneously and say, "Why you no scream, *viva!*" then, giggle. We turn to the salesgirl, "Alright, we'll go figure it out and come back to pay you."

Kim and I go to the money exchange place not expecting the Don Juan of the Riviera Maya will serve us. He approaches and his smile eases my anxiety instantly. What a face and body to behold! Did we walk into a photo shoot by mistake? He looks like a model straight out of a GQ magazine: linen slacks, European loafers, white shirt unbuttoned low, classy, white-framed GQ glasses. Kim sounds a low "meow," our signal a guy is hot, and I laugh nervously. "Can I help you ladies?" he asks.

Yes, you can become my Latin lover. How about starting tonight? I think, but shyly say, "I have a problem." I try to tell him my tale of woe in an expressive, dramatic way and when he laughs, I think, *You laugh now, but you won't be laughing when I kiss you later!*

Kim sees I'm losing, if not lost, the battle to be cool, so she takes over as protective big sister and we somehow end up in his conference room where he persuades me to open an account. Next, I have to deposit all the travelers' checks into it. This means I have to sign all two-hundred checks again in two places. *What a freakin' pain in the ass! Whose brilliant idea was it to bring travelers' checks, anyway? (Um, that would be mine.)* I send Kim out to shop, for I've already done this drill: it will take two hours again. When that's done, GQ helps me transfer thirteen-thousand dollars over to L'Autre du Monde.

"How do you want your seven-thousand dollars cash back?" He asks.

I'm still not thinking at all, I'm spinning with infatuation and almost cross-eyed from the signing, so I say, "Just write me a check for seven-thousand dollars."

"Okay, you'll need to go cash it at our bank down the street."

I meet up with Kim and together we go to his bank to cash my check. I'm thinking that the small, Dooney & Bourke backpack I'm wearing can be used to carry the cash back to my condo, where we will pop it into my safe. When we get to the bank, we see the line is out the door. It is the second Friday of the month—*payday*! We get in line, at least thirty local citizens in front of us, and wait for an hour. As two white *señoritas*; one blond and one redhead, we stick out like sore thumbs. And as Mexicans here often have Mayan ancestry and so are short, Kim and I tower over everyone. Never mind that, about a half hour into it, we both realize we have to use the restroom. That will have to wait, cuz I am not moving from this line!

When we are finally first in line and I ask the teller for approximately seventy thousand pesos, this creates quite a stir behind the teller's window. They whisper and giggle and point to us *gringas* and it looks like it might be an issue for us to get that much cash. The teller goes and gets the bank manager, and there's all this hustle and bustle, and scurrying going on behind the teller window. Kim and I just stand there giggling and looking around at people staring at us. What a scene; it's funny and yet not so funny wondering if we'll ever get my money.

The teller and manager finally hustle up stacks and stacks of pesos. Kim and I stuff my backpack but cannot close the latch. It is bulging with money. Obviously, I cannot wear it on my back, so, I bear-hug it, leaning over it like a Mama bear protecting her threatened cub.

Kim body guards me as we make a run for it out of the bank. She's prepared to play "clean-up" in case any wads of money fall out of the backpack. We jostle our way past the people in line and push open the front door. The people's facial expressions say: *What are those stupid gringas doing? They are muy loco (very crazy).*

I want to say, "Hey, we're just a couple of white chicks making a bank heist in Mexico, what's all the fuss about?" *Bonnie and Clyde... Brookie and Kim... Hmmmm, kinda has a nice ring to it.*

We scurry down the road, Kim waving madly to the nearest taxi and we jump in before we're arrested. I'm even nervous about the taxi driver taking us somewhere, killing us and taking all the money! He, of course, doesn't know my Dooney & Bourke backpack is stuffed full of money.

When the driver guns the car and we are pushed back against the seat, Kim and I look at each other and simultaneously cry, "We win!"

Chapter 24

SLEEPLESS IN SEA GRASS

THAT FIRST NIGHT, WE ARE MINUS A FEW ESSENTIALS—NO COOK-ware or beds or couch cushions. Because we have no pots and pans, we have to utilize a hibachi on the balcony for cooking. The couches made of sea grass—a kind of hard, woven wicker—arrive minus their cushions. The cushions have to be custom made and will be delivered in a couple of weeks.

We've stashed all but a day's allotment of pesos into the safe and with a few, go buy some fish to cook on the hibachi. The mosquitos are out in force, humming around our balcony, so we set up a circle of six citronella candles all around us as we cook. There we are, two women, six buckets of citronella, sitting in the dark cooking our dinner. People on well-lit balconies seem to be staring at us, and we get to giggling as we imagine what they might be thinking.

"I bet they think we're witches, performing some kind of ritual with the circle of candles," Kim says.

I laugh. "Yes, we're keeping the evil spirits away and everyone knows the name of the evil spirits in these parts is— Mosquito! Let's chant something to keep them away!" I add.

"Yes, yes," Kim agrees. "I'm fluent in Pig Latin," she says and we start in, forcing our voices into lower registers, drawing out the words like slow, ominous incantations: "Osquito-may, osquito-may. Osquito may, ogay, away!" Then we giggle in high-pitched, trilling voices, sounding like witches (or fools, I'm sure.)

That night we hunker down to sleep on the cushion-less couches. Oh, that sea grass is hard and as comfortable as a plank. Even the two, twelve-by-twelve-inch throw pillows we squeeze beneath our torsos, don't help—they just become lumps. Sleep eludes us.

When the beds arrive the next day without the mattresses, Kim calls up our sweet British saleslady at L'Autre du Monde. Repressing her frustration she asks, "*Dónde están* the mattresses?"

The British saleslady must have given Kim the wrong answer because she said, "Correction, the mattresses will be delivered *today*!"

She hangs up, tired and yet relieved and announces, "We'll get some sleep tonight."

Still nothing can completely spoil the win of taking possession of my very own vacation home in a place and time I would never have imagined eighteen months ago when I thought my world was falling apart.

Chapter 25

Hot and Stinky

IN JULY, I GO BACK TO PLAYA BY MYSELF WITH A LONG LIST OF TASKS that need to get done. The first on the list concerns security. In June, we had ordered mini-blinds that were due to be installed in July. I need them because there are no curtains over the windows, so no privacy. By now I've got furniture and a big TV and people can look into the condo.

Wow, it is freaking hot in Playa in July!

I am looking forward to relaxing in my new condo with a cold beer and some yummy chicken for dinner. When Kim and I were here in June, we baked some chicken breasts (after we finally got some cookware) and froze them in anticipation of my returning in a month. But when I arrive, Friday afternoon, I find that there's no power in my condominium. *WTF?* That means no A/C, no lights and no refrigeration. Did I mention that it was hoooooooot, hot, hot, hot? Seeing that it's late Friday afternoon, no businesses are open. The electric company, the manager and Guapo—everybody's gone for the weekend. And so I spend the first three days in my condo with no AC in the most sweltering July heat I've ever endured.

Is paradise turning into hell?

I open up all the doors and all the windows trying to catch the breeze coming in from the sea. The breeze, however, comes with a slew of mosquitos. *Man the mosquitos are big and beefy down here.* And I do not have screens for my doors and windows yet. So, I have to choose between sauna-level heat and big carnivorous insects. I suck it up and decide, *Okay. I'll put bug spray on, and I'll pray.*

And did I mention my refrigerator is not working because there's no power? When I open it, even the crack that I do, I am hit with a stench that out-stinks a combo of garbage, sewage and a high school boys' locker room. Everything I had left in there has been rotting for I don't know how long. Grrrrr. I shut it in a hurry. There isn't much I can do in the dark. In fact, I really can't stay here and enjoy it because there's no electricity to watch TV or to read. *I better get out of here for a while.*

I decide to go drown my sorrows at my favorite Argentinian steak-house, just down the street. Oddly, they make the best pizza I have ever tasted! Who knew Argentinians were masters of pizza? I think their secret is in the cheese. Luckily, I had purchased a cooler when I was here in June, so I buy some ice on the way home, and put my leftovers in my makeshift refrigerator when I get back to my condo. Then, I hear some people talking outside, so I walk out onto my balcony and see one of my neighbors, whom I have not yet met.

He's a handsome young man with a contagious laugh, a genuine smile, perhaps around mid-thirties. He's cooking dinner with another guy who looks to be a friend of his, and when they come back out on their balcony, I say, "Hey, how's it going?"

"Hey. Good. How are you?" he asks. They appear to be Americans, so there's no language problem. We introduce ourselves and I tell him my sad story of no power, excessive heat and beefy mosquitos.

He goes, "Come on down, we're having dinner."

And I say, "No, thanks, I just ate."

"Come on down anyway, I've got air conditioning."

"Okay, I'll be right down!"

So I go over and spend a few refreshing hours with them. Then he walks me home and brings his flashlight to see if he can tell what's going on with the power. His friend comes with us because he is curious to see a penthouse unit.

My new neighbor's very nice and there's clearly some energy between us. He cannot find any cause for my power being out, so we all three decide to enjoy the moonlight and fresh breeze on my balcony and share a bottle of wine. It's actually kind of romantic, and I can't help but think, *maybe this is once again serendipity lending me a hand; the strangest of events occurring to bring two people together.* After the wine is gone and there is nothing more to say, I am kind of thinking he is going to plant a kiss on me; but instead he jumps up and says, "I'll be back tomorrow when it's daylight and I can see more." Then he and his friend leave me to enjoy the rest of the evening in my dark condo on my own, with a flashlight that's gone a bit dim. *What is with the guys in Playa? Am I that intimidating? Am I that undesirable? Hmmm… I clearly misread that one!*

Fast forward to the next day, when My Good Neighbor as I will refer to him, comes back over and he opens everything up in my refrigerator; it was epic. Everything had rotted.

He's emphatic, "You've *got* to get all this stuff out of here *now.*" He puts a second pair of my dishwashing gloves on and hands me the first. He helps me pull everything out of the freezer and the fridge and throws it away, plastic containers and all. There are many science experiments—everything has blue, green or pink mold growing on it; you can see it through the containers. If I had wanted something romantic to happen between us, my hopes are now sufficiently squashed. This activity was about as romantic as cleaning toilets together.

Getting the smell out of my brand new refrigerator and freezer takes me days. I scrub it with bleach for hours each day. The smell doesn't fully vanish, and I'm sick. I am starting to think I am going to have to buy a brand new refrigerator to replace my brand new refrigerator. *Shit.*

Monday morning, I ask Guapo to walk down to the electric company with me to find out what happened—to inquire why I don't have any power.

They tell me in Spanish, "Yeah, you didn't pay your bill, so we shut your electricity off."

"What bill?"

And they say, "Oh, yes. You should have your bill—it should be in your condo."

Down in Playa, I'm told, the electric company bills you every other month. And the way they do it is they slip the bills under your door. *What??* Well, I guess that makes sense because they don't even have mailboxes down here! So, of course, residing in Colorado, I could not retrieve my bills from underneath my door!

Nice wake up call to the new routine. Part of taking risks is learning how to anticipate what's required of you and the problems that might arise in that risky undertaking. Boy, am I naïve—as if paradise would be devoid of bills! I am reminded that my dream home is in a "developing" country and I have to figure out how to retrieve and pay the bills when I am not in Playa.

That brings me to a vivid epiphany: *Everybody who owns a place down here and yet doesn't live here really needs a local property manager for just these sorts of things. I need to interview property managers and hire one as soon as possible.*

For now, I have to go back home to do some contract work, so I can afford to pay these bills and to finance the next trip down here. In August I will come back to finish decorating and buying furniture. It will be the grand unveiling of my little slice of paradise, as we plan a vacation for a small group of us!

Chapter 26

Don't Look Now, a Hurricane's A-Comin'

THE AUGUST TRIP IS THE FINAL DECORATING AND LOGISTICS TRIP—
getting everything ready to go. The finish line at last! We plan to celebrate by just kicking back and enjoying my dream house. I decide to go down first, then Kim will join me for the second week and her boyfriend, Quatro, will join us for the last four or five days. We've also invited Quatro's nephew and his girlfriend.

When I arrive, I look like a Sherpa. I've got so many extra duffel bags and suitcases full of linens and towels, kitchen things like "The Rabbit" wine bottle opener (my favorite kitchen tool) and other things I was afraid I wouldn't be able to find in Mexico. I wonder how others view me as I schlep up three flights of stairs to the condo. Some people might think I'm a witch (from the night Kim and I held our candlelight patio ceremony), others might see me as a high-end bag lady, who knows? I'm laughing at myself, thinking about it. The first few days, I'm extremely busy with minutia.

When Kim arrives, we start to interview property managers. After the electric bill debacle, I have every intention of hiring one. I am shocked. The rates they're charging are astronomical. They charge forty to fifty percent of the owner's rental revenues. I feel like saying, *are you crazy!?!* *In the United States, it's like ten to twenty percent.*

Kim and I both conclude that this is highway robbery. That's when the wheels start turning—my brain goes into overdrive and I start firing off thoughts. "This is not rocket science, Kim. I could live down here and start a property management business. I could charge, well, tops thirty percent and probably still make plenty of money. And I could give the homeowner a better deal instead of ripping them off. I'd be providing a valuable service, and my competitive advantage would be that I'm an experienced American businesswoman. I could target English-speaking American and Canadian clients who own properties here. And because I am English speaking, I will gain instant credibility and trust with the Americans and the Canadians." I stop to take a breath.

Kim is dumbstruck. Then she laughs, "Who is this woman? Hear her roar!"

Despite the setbacks of my last trip, I'm still enamored with Playa del Carmen. I'm thinking, *Oh, how exciting and thrilling to start a new life in a new country doing something totally new.*

Kim says, "With your background in finance, you could learn property management in a snap."

"Well, I've been looking for something to do that would excite me and this just might be it!"

🍥 🍥 🍥

As Kim and I scurry around preparing for the arrival of our guests, we suddenly get the bad news that will foil all our plans.

Hurricane Dean is headed our way! And it's a big one.

Not only do we have to monitor a Category 5 hurricane, but we have to warn Kim's boyfriend, Quatro, and his nephew so they will not come down here. Kim and I have not yet figured out how to efficiently make telephone calls to the United States. We are using calling cards and we are not having much success connecting to the airlines, or to Quatro. This communication hurdle becomes a major obstacle for us.

While we are trying to figure out how to get through to Quatro, I get this strange desire to stay here through Hurricane Dean. I think it would be kind of exciting to witness a hurricane first hand and see what it is like. It would also be cool to have a survival story of having lived through one. Further, I feel a very maternalistic feeling about my condo and want to hold it close. But I decide to keep this desire secret because it's a frowned-upon urge and also, I need to think about Kim's safety.

It becomes clear that Hurricane Dean is headed straight for us, and we're going to have to cut our trip short and leave early. But how to get hold of Quatro to tell him a hurricane is approaching so he won't come down here?

After many failed attempts with the calling cards, we finally find an internet and phone café—and Kim attempts to call him, but he is not answering. She leaves him message after message, and this goes on for twenty-four hours. Now she's in a panic and cries, "Oh my God. Where *is* he? Why isn't he calling us back?"

I've never seen Kim so alarmed and restless. An impending hurricane alone can make one feel a bit helpless, but not being able to find a loved one is nerve-racking. "It's almost time for him to head for the airport," Kim frets.

"Speaking of which, we still need to change our flights," I try to keep my voice calm. Who knows how many other people are bombarding the airlines to do the same thing? This is our first experience running from Mother Nature and we are both *rattled*.

The day goes on and we watch the entire town prepare for the hurricane. We are fascinated by the process they go through to get ready for a giant storm; boarding up storefronts, windows, and even moving my rooftop mechanical equipment into a little housing structure. Meanwhile, in a matter of hours, the interior of my spectacular condo starts to look like a thrift store—patio furniture, among other things, piled up everywhere. It's downright unsettling.

I dissolve into tears thinking about leaving my condo in what likely will be the rough hands of Mother Nature. *Oh my God, I'm going to lose everything, and I just got it done!* Now, I'm worried sick too—about what the hurricane will do to my dream house.

Finally, Kim gets a hold of Quatro, and finds out that he's been in a car accident. The entire time she was trying to reach him, he's been in the hospital, and his phone was still in his car. So anyway, he's having his own drama at home, and now her fear has given way to relief and concern for him. Kim's stuck in Mexico, Quatro is in the hospital, my dream home is in danger, and we have to evacuate *now*.

At the last minute, we are able to book a flight and get home before the hurricane hits.

I'm disappointed about our trip—and I'm just *sick* about what's going on in my beloved Playa. By now, I've really bonded with my special place; its people, restaurants, shops and the beaches. I watch the weather channel for twenty-four hours straight from my couch in Colorado, crying helplessly as I watch Hurricane Dean's destruction. I'm consumed with these thoughts: *My dream come true is about to get washed away. It's just another thing that I can't control. Another thing that I may lose.*

I'm reminded once again how temporal life can be.

PART FOUR

Taking Massive, Decisive Action – Paradise Calling

೧ ೧ ೧

It is not because things are difficult that we do not dare,
it is because we do not dare that they are difficult.

~ Seneca ~

Chapter 27

The Magic of a One-Way Ticket

PLAYA IS EVACUATED, AND I FINALLY GET HOLD OF GUAPO, MY builder. To my relief, it seems that the eye of the hurricane skirted Playa, but we are not sure what destruction my complex endured. Guapo says, "I'll check on your condo as soon as I can get back there." But he doesn't get back to Playa right away. Many days later, I finally hear that my condo is fine. Whew!

One would think the hurricane would dampen my desire to go live and work in Playa del Carmen, but it doesn't. I start researching and learning property management on my own as soon as I know my Playa is safe.

In addition to self-study in property management at home in Colorado from September to December, I put all the legitimate elements of a new business in place. I now have a business plan, business model, an LLC set up, a website, brochures, a logo, business cards and I've completed the market research. I send out emails to all the home owners in my condo complex. *I should start with some clients in my own building. First of all, I already have that connection. Second, I'll be living there in the same building, so can keep a watchful eye over their units.* I get several inquiries back, but only procure one client from those emails.

I need to rent out my house in Colorado in order to financially pull off moving to Playa. But by December first, I still have no renters. I need to make something happen, so I take a leap of faith and buy a one-way ticket to Cancun. *One way, wow!* The ticket is for January 6, three days before my birthday. I'm getting more and more daring with taking risks, and it pays off. Within a few days, I have my renter! The only thing is, they need to move in right away, so I have to vacate my home three weeks before my departure date. Guess who comes to the rescue? Yup, my loyal and lovely friend Kim, of course. I move into her basement bedroom for my three remaining weeks in Denver. I have a very long list of things I have to do in order to move to a foreign country. Of course, I store most of my wardrobe, as I will be living in flip flops, swimsuits, shorts and tees, an occasional skirt and sunscreen from now on. New wardrobe, new lifestyle, new life; how exhilarating!

Another piece of the puzzle I need to put in place is this: Until I become fluent in Spanish, I will need a right-hand person who's bilingual. I remember the lovely Latina I met about a year ago in my yoga teacher training class. She has a college degree in marketing, is bilingual and I think she'd be the perfect person to work for me while I'm becoming fluent. I think by now she has probably moved back to Playa del Carmen.

I contact her via email, and sure enough, she's interested. She doesn't happen to be working, she's looking for a new career, she wants to do something a little more personal than working in a large marketing department of a hotel or a resort and so she is game. We agree to meet in January, shortly after I arrive, to set things up.

With everything seemingly done for my big move, I go to a Christmas party at the company for which I am still doing contract work. Some of the men I talk to (many of whom have done risky and amazing things in their own lives) are awestruck when I tell them I'm moving to Mexico and intend to start a new business there. When they ask, "How did you do that, how did you pull it off?" I answer, "I don't know, I just decided to do it and made it happen." As I say these words, I realize that this could become a kind of mantra: *Decide to do it, make it happen.* I smile, pleased with myself.

The Magic of a One-Way Ticket

The magic that comes from buying that one-way ticket surprises me. It means much more to me than a plane ride to Mexico. It represents my ticket to freedom and adventure. I have found a place I've fallen in love with and if I choose to never come back I don't have to; I have no return trip to dread!

Hello? I'm on a one-way ticket to Paradise, folks. Literally!

Chapter 28

New Wardrobe, New Lifestyle, No Problem

I'M HEEEERE!!! WHEN I ARRIVE IN PLAYA, I HIT THE GROUND RUNNING to get the infrastructure of the business set up. The first thing I do is sign up for intensive Spanish lessons. The second thing I do is meet with my Latina friend. We go over my business plan and the logistics of working together. The expectation is that she will be my reliable, right-hand helper. In February, there's going to be a real estate trade show in Playa, and I decide to get a booth to quickly ramp-up the business and solicit new clients. She is enthusiastic about our collaboration and intends to help me a great deal preparing for and working at the booth. We both agree that, at the trade show, everything we show and do has to have the message, "We are here and we are open for business!"

❧ ❧ ❧

Today is my birthday—and My Right-Hand Latina is the only friend I have in Playa at this point, so she and I go to dinner. And where do you suppose I choose to have my birthday dinner? Yup, my favorite restaurant in Playa, La Parilla. I, of course, order nachos and a large margarita. But this isn't just any large margarita. Little did I know the *large* margaritas are served in a yard glass. We bust out laughing when we see it coming to the table. This glass is so tall; I have to set it on the ground to reach my very tall straw. "*Quiero ver el gran jefe terminar su trago!* (I want to see the big boss finish her big drink!)" snorts My Right-Hand Latina.

"No way, José! Lest I'll be your drunk *el jefe*," is the best I can manage in Spanish. "How do you say straw in Spanish?"

"*Paja*," she replies.

"What?"

"*Paja*."

"Spell it."

"*Pe-a-jota-a*."

"Oh dear. Becoming fluent in Spanish might be a little harder than I was anticipating." I wave the waiter over. "*Masero*, can I have another 'pa-ha' *por favor*?" He looks at me quizzically. I point to my very tall straw and say, "*Una mas*," smiling. He chuckles and turns away to fetch another *paja* so my Right-Hand Latina can help me drink my *grande* margarita. And without knowing it, my first Spanish lesson was born—the art of pointing and smiling.

We cover more logistics over dinner. One of the urgent tasks is to find someone to clean the condos. We also talk about my one client, how he is in the middle of decorating his condo, and we agree to the client's request that we oversee his interior designer. This is not usually part of the property manager's role, but I decide to go the extra mile because he's my first client and I want to be all about customer service. I also hope to get referrals from him.

ۉ ۉ ۉ

The next order of business is to hire a Mexican business attorney. There are a million things to do to start a business, but what are all the complexities with starting one in another country? I need to find these legalities out, pronto. I start asking around for a good business attorney.

In the meantime, because I need to learn Spanish to better understand the laws, culture and mentality of this country and based on my clear lack of grasping Spanish 101 at my birthday dinner, I concentrate on my Spanish language lessons.

Chapter 29

Mi Maestro

I TOOK EIGHT YEARS OF SPANISH IN SCHOOL—FROM FOURTH THROUGH eleventh grade. I'll never forget my eighth grade teacher, Señora Ruiz, with her one-inch, bright red nails. She would tap those nails on the side of her face as she pondered the next thing she was going to say, "*Entonces... despues...,*" which loosely translates to "so, next." Anyway, I always made As and Bs in Spanish, despite being distracted by her dazzling nails!

Now that I am in Playa, I figure all that Spanish instruction is going to come right back—just like riding a bike. Right? I think, *I'll take a few lessons and soon I'll be fluent because I'm immersed in the culture, speaking it all the time.* Confident of my abilities, I sign up for group lessons in the academy. That class offers instruction for newbies, but I think I'll advance quickly up to intermediate. Wrong! I'm sitting in the beginners' class for the first week, and they are so far over my head, I'm not keeping up—at all!

This is *not* easy, this is *not* coming back to me, and I'm completely lost. I immediately shift gears and tell them, "I need private instruction because I'm not keeping up. I need to go back to the beginning." That's when they assign a private tutor to me.

For two months, I go every other day for an hour and a half—fairly intensive. Mi Maestro is a musician at heart and a big flirt. I keep wondering if he will ask me out, but then he reveals one day that he's married. Nevertheless, there is still some harmless, enjoyable sexy vibration underlying our communication. He's great fun and we laugh as much as we learn—mostly at me, how I'm talking like a second grader in Spanish because I only know present tense! We are working on past tense; but I default back to present tense, clinging to it like a child to her mother's leg. "The Power of Now!" I say, quoting Eckhart Tolle's popular book title from 2004. "The power of now!" is my defense for only speaking in the present tense. My instructor has no clue what I'm referring to!

Mi Maestro makes learning fun by taking me places that bring the language to life. We go out on Fifth Avenue, the main street, and talk about everyday activities of life. We go to a restaurant and use Spanish to talk about furniture, dishes, food and about the people walking by. Playa becomes our first classroom alternated with some instruction time at the Institute.

As is typical in Playa, there is always construction going on, for the town is growing. They start building a hotel right next door to the little institute where I am taking my lessons. Jackhammers drown out the instruction, so Mi Maestro suggests we go to my condo for the next couple of weeks. I think, *Hmmmm, I don't know about that.* But as it is hot elsewhere, we end up going to my air-conditioned condo. I just decide I'm a grown woman. If he makes a move, I can fend him off!

It's going to be okay, he's professional. When we work in my condo, Mi Maestro uses my surroundings to teach me more things about everyday life: views from the condo, hosting guests at the condo, and various rooms in the condo. However I am adamant about avoiding bedroom topics! We also play the game "concentration." You know, the game where you turn two cards over, and if you match them, you pick them up; if you don't, you turn them back over, and try to remember where they are so that you can eventually match as many cards as possible. He teaches me game procedure in Spanish. For example, I learn the Spanish for, *whose turn is it?* He also has a deck of cards with objects depicted on them to help learn vocabulary. Perhaps of most value to me in conversing with the locals is learning how to say, "More slowly please." (*Mas lento por favor.*) I might have said that a few thousand times while in Playa!

If I know I have to run an errand that day, I ask Mi Maestro, How do I say "such and such" in Spanish? I write it down and when I get to my destination, pull out my notes, give my listener a sheepish grin and read my question. They love it, down here, if you even attempt to speak their language. I just have to repeat my favorite, *Mas lento por favor, yo aprendiendo Español.* (More slowly, please. I am learning Spanish.) They are so accommodating and gracious. When I tell them I am still learning Spanish, they talk back to me as if I am a child, which is a good thing!

No matter what, it's rewarding to speak with the locals; I really feel a sense of increasing connection. They know I want to relate to them on their terms, and they reciprocate. I am reminded of Batman's declaration: "I'm not learning Spanish! They can speak *my* language." In contrast to this attitude, I am grateful to be learning the secrets of their language and delighted with the people teaching me, such as my sweet, lively tutor.

I also watch a lot of captioned television and listen to Latin music, hoping to pick up some Spanish from there. The captions flash across the screen pretty fast, so you have to be a fast reader to learn via television. Through these informal channels of learning Spanish, I discover there are three handy little tips that had I known early on, would have made my progress go a lot faster: 1) every single letter is pronounced in a word in Spanish, 2) the same word is used for many different things, meaning there's really less vocabulary to learn, and 3) the letters "*mente*" added to the end of almost any word gives you an adverb—for example, exactly = *exactamente.*

After intensive lessons and lots of time logged with my television and my iPod, I am still a novice, always asking my tutor annoying questions like, "Why is 'table' feminine?" Little by little I make progress and advance. I no longer speak Spanish like a second grader, I speak it as well as a lively, eager, third grader! Hey, that's progress!

Chapter 30

UNDER THE RADAR

L ET THE DRAMA BEGIN! THE MEXICAN ATTORNEY I HIRE ADVISES me that it's very expensive to do business in Mexico and tells me in so many words *not* to do it legally! *What?* My jaw drops. He continues to matter-of-factly tell me I need to fly under the radar until I get big enough that it's impossible to fly under the radar. Did I mention that it appears that a lawyer is counseling me to *break* the law?!

Oh my God. What am I getting myself into?

He goes on, "Small businesses pay tax on their top-line revenue and their bottom-line net profit. And you are required to provide your employees a housing allowance and fifteen percent of the net profits in addition to healthcare benefits."

This guy is blowing my mind!

"By the way, you should pay your employees partly under the table in cash and partly legitimately by check. That way the workers don't have to pay income taxes on the under-the-table cash and you don't have to pay payroll taxes on the under-the-table cash either." He concludes, "Everyone does it. Otherwise you cannot afford to do business down here."

Holy shit! Are you freakin' kidding me?

I now understand what I am up against. It sounds dang near impossible for small businesses to make money down in Mexico. Now I get why everybody, it seems, does business under the radar and against the rules. I also realize that it's a real burden for employers to have employees because they have to pay them all those perks and extras. I'm starting to think that contract workers may be the way to go. I need to have a little chat with my Right-Hand Latina. The attorney does, however, advise me to follow the rules just enough to look legitimate. *Oh, so it's okay to be half a crook? Isn't that sort of like being half-pregnant?* Growing up in America, you're told to obey the laws of the land and to pay Uncle Sam, lest there are consequences. Big, ugly, undesirable legal consequences. My parents also taught me all my life, "Be honest and follow the rules."

But now I'm being told, "No, no. Your survival depends on your *not* following the rules." Will I compromise, now? This is a real pickle for me.

Doing a bit of soul searching on the subject of honesty, I have to admit to myself that I am not always thoroughly and completely honest. For instance, while not overtly deceptive, when it has to do with my mother, I am often less than forthcoming. I justify this, saying that I give her partial truths that will prevent her from worrying because she is such a worry-wart. I learn this as I grow older and wiser; that if Mom would worry herself sick about something I might be doing, I'll tell her that "something" after the fact, if at all. Moving to Mexico comes to mind.

Speaking of which, now I have to find a way to tell my parents I'm in Mexico without telling them I've moved here. I have to find a truth that's acceptable to them.

My parents are not going to be able to call my home phone and get me; instead they are going to get some stranger who's renting my house. So I tell them I'm just going to spend some time down in Playa to get my business set up, and then I'll be back home. (Which is not a lie.) My plan is to give this experiment in Mexico a year, but my parents will not know that I'm also living here. They will think I'm just spending an awful lot of time down in Mexico. So that is how I con my parents.

The whole thing about flying under the radar, however, still has me unnerved. I can't quite wrap my brain around what to do. What it seems to come down to is a different work ethic or maybe different views on what comprises ethical business practice. What's similar to both the U.S. and Mexico is the desire to make a business survive and thrive—but I am about to find out how different our ways of operating are to make that happen! I'm beginning to see that visiting paradise and living here are two very different things, indeed.

Although I am discouraged, I am not deterred. *Somebody down here must be making money.* I've already transplanted myself here; I must make a go of it. I am reminded of my decision to move to Mexico when I hadn't a clue as to how I was going to make it happen. Nonetheless, I just decided to do it and made it happen. Yeah, that's my new mantra: *Decide to do it, then just make it happen!*

Rah-rah aside, I also notice I'm not feeling very good physically. Maybe it's the stress of my new business reality. But I more or less ignore it and plunge ahead planning a business which will grow so big that one day, it will have to be conducted above the radar.

And now I am ready to immerse myself in my new country: the culture, the strange business laws and the people. And the people, as it turns out, consist of both Mexicans and expats.

Chapter 31

DESTINY, FANTASY, REALITY

W E ARE HAVING THE FIRST ANNUAL HOMEOWNERS' MEETING FOR our condominium this morning. Although most owners took possession of their units last year, it apparently takes a while to formally organize the homeowners' association. I am eager to actively partici- pate in my community and what better way than via the homeowners' association? Not long after the meeting begins, I notice this young, handsome, athletic man who is active in the meeting. We immediately become friendly—partly because he's American and is one of the few English-speaking people at the meeting.

The intent of the first annual meeting is to elect a "vigilance com- mittee" (board of directors) made up of homeowners and to establish the rules and regulations. Ideally, there should be as many homeowners present as possible at this meeting. However, our homeowners are notified of the first annual meeting via a note slipped under their doors. Sound familiar? Needless to say, most homeowners never knew about the meeting since they don't reside down here full-time.

I call this attractive man, "Athlete." The way that he conducts himself in that first meeting impresses me. "First order of business," he says to the representatives of the management company, "until we have the capability of using modern technology for meetings such as conference calls, Skype or video calls, you need to send emails out to the homeown- ers—because they don't live here and won't see the notes under their doors! If you email a homeowner, and they want to attend the meeting, they can fly here for it."

"Yes, but, what if we want to change the time or the day of the meeting?" someone asks. "We do that quite often."

I speak up, "Well, we can't do that. People buy plane tickets and take time off from work. We can't just change the time of the meeting!"

Athlete and I look at each other, incredulous at their unsophistication. In his eyes is a hint of admiration for me, I think. In that meeting, I get elected to the vigilance committee. Of course, that was no real honor: They needed three homeowners for the committee and since only three homeowners showed up, I was elected!

Keep in mind that I am still convinced that I may be drawn to Playa to meet Mr. Right. *Oh, maybe this is my destiny! Maybe Athlete is my destiny,* I think, as I size him up. We hang out a little bit initially—he's bilingual and is helpful in working out logistics. For example, he puts me in touch with people who come to build the bug screens for my windows and doors.

We flirt, but the flirtation is short-lived. He has a girlfriend, for one thing, and he runs hot and cold with me for another. This is disconcerting and I introvert a bit—easy to do after being burned so deeply—those scars still linger. So I think, *is it me, or is it his flaw? As a romantic, am I doomed to disappointment?*

I tell myself, *Brooke, keep focused here. You've got a business to promote and to run and a language to learn!*

So, I immediately turn my attention back to looking for additional clients. I go to several meetings with people and give them proposals. I also need to buckle down to get ready for the upcoming trade show. It's a big step for my business and is very expensive—three-thousand dollars to rent booth space—but I feel it is necessary to garner more clients. I guess I'll just have to channel my sexual and romantic longings into work for a while. I sure haven't found my destiny in that department yet. Sigh.

PART FIVE
Getting Back in the Game – Making New Connections

❧ ❧ ❧

When we know ourselves to be connected to all others,
acting compassionately is simply the natural thing to do.

~ Rachel Naomi Remen ~

Chapter 32

Tres Amigas & The Super Bowl

FEBRUARY IS WILD! IT BRINGS AN UNEXPECTED WHIRLWIND OF AC-tivity and surprising encounters with many intriguing, captivating people. If I were to describe February's emotional atmosphere; it ranges from celebration, agitation, excitement, astonishment to passionate.

The parade of people begins the first week of February when my partner-in-crime, Kim, and Kim's friend, Sarah, visit me in my new home. Sarah has never been to Mexico before, so this is a pretty big deal for her.

Because I'm getting ready for my trade-show and establishing my business, I'm busy the whole time they are here with appointments and trade show preparation. Kim and Sarah spend a lot of time together without me, but one of the things I do create with them is a Super Bowl party at my condo. It is the most improvised and funniest party I've ever given!

Somebody tells us about a place in the heart of Playa where you can get rotisserie chickens that are very good. This place is over by the bank (of bank heist fame) in a part of town I'm not that familiar with, so I'm a little nervous to be traipsing around there, just us *tres amigas*.

We walk around and around looking for it until we finally see this crazy-looking outdoor restaurant with chicken wire for walls. Our reward for finding the place—*it is the best chicken we've ever had in our entire lives!* They cut the chicken down the breastbone, pound it flat, and then grill it like that. I call it "smashed chicken" because that's exactly what it looks like. They put together a whole packaged dinner to go, everything you need: tortillas, salsa, beans and rice, along with the amazing smashed chicken. And all that—the chicken and all the sides, for only $7.50! We buy several chickens and all the trimmings and then start walking home. We're clowning around, very attuned to one another's senses of humor. Three white chicks with three brown chickens; all we need is three French hens, two turtle doves, etc. We sing the "Twelve days of Christmas," laughing all the way to the beach and then decide we need a refreshment.

We sit down at one of the dozens of bars/restaurants dotting the beach and each order a beer, whereby we are informed *no hay cerveza hoy* (there is no beer today). *What??* "Why not?" we ask.

"Because tomorrow is our election day in Mexico and by law we cannot sell alcohol twenty-four hours prior to when the voting starts."

Incredulous, we stand up, thank the *masero*, take our chickens and start heading back to the condo. Not really fathoming that they won't sell alcohol the day before the Super Bowl and not really believing that every store will follow the letter of the law, we stop at several markets to see if we can get the necessary alcohol for the party. Although businesses seem to selectively follow the law in Mexico, apparently this is one law they *all* choose to follow. Playa is dried up. Unbelievable!

We guess that officials don't want the populace drunk at the polls. I don't know if it's local or national. But, the point relevant to our party is, they prohibit alcohol twenty-four hours before the elections, which means we're not going to have any alcohol for the Super Bowl party! We've told our guests we'd provide the food, and asked people to BYOB. But if we hadn't known about the twenty-four hour prohibition, we think nobody else will. They'll be going to the store soon to get alcohol, and there won't be any for sale. With any luck—and it's a pretty strong possibility—people will have plenty of alcohol already on hand and this won't be an issue.

When we get back to the condo, we check to see what alcohol I have lying around. Sometimes renters leave behind leftover bottles, and sure enough we find some leftover peach vodka in the freezer (from when I rented my condo out over Christmastime)! Never in a million years would I buy peach vodka, but at least it's something. What the hell are we going to do with peach vodka? Then Sarah comes up with the bright idea to make Jell-O shots out of our peach vodka. I haven't had Jell-O shots in twenty-five years; but how festive for our little party!

I have invited a very eclectic group of people whom I've met during my first month in Playa. Most of them are neighbors in my condo. Athlete brings his girlfriend—*okay, he really does have a girlfriend!*—and a semi-pro golfer friend of his. Another neighbor towers over us. He's a six-foot, seven inches, bleached-blond, spiky-haired man from Transylvania, Romania. Yes, Transylvania! Who knew there really was such a place? We invite another English-speaking, Mormon neighbor who brings his visiting father. The good thing about Playa is that people don't miss a good party. So, my English-speaking, Mormon neighbor invites a few of his friends, as well. All in, there are about twelve of us at my first party.

One of the most inviting features of the condo is the large kitchen window near the front door. It provides a fishbowl view of the interior, and happens to slide open, which causes it to take on a life of its own on this particular evening. So, the Tres Amigas are busy preparing for our party, when our first guest appears outside the kitchen and quips, "Is this a drive-through window? I'd like to place an order, please. Some chicken and a beer to go."

And voila, "Brooke's Drive-Through" is born.

The party is a hit, what with a lively pack of expats, the random mix of alcohol from who-knows-where, and a football game as the excuse du jour. There's singing, dancing and cigar-smoking on the roof. Oh yeah, and Jell-O shots!

Kim and Sarah later recount the pro-golfer's concern when he saw their twin beds in the second bedroom, "How does this work?" he says.

They look at each other perplexed and he continues… "I mean, what do you *do?*"

"Do?"

"How do you hook up when one of you brings someone home from the bar?"

He is answered by a roar of laughter from two girls who find man's biggest concerns enlightening.

"Let's go back to Brooke's Drive-Through for another Jell-O shot," Sarah says and the group rejoins the party.

After the party, the three of us debrief. Kim says, "All your friends are fun and nice, but I've never seen so many wonderful wackos all in one place before!"

Sarah adds, "Yeah, fascinating men, but every one of them has a screw loose!" We laugh and then I sigh, "I guess I need to expand my pool of male prospects if I want to find a Prince Charming with all his screws intact!"

"Yes, and make sure he can screw well, too!" We all think this is hysterically funny—shows you what Jell-O shots can do to one's brain!

There's something amusing and magical about us three girls together in Playa. When the week is over, Sarah moans that she doesn't want to leave. "It's the first time I've ever been on vacation where I'm not just dying to get home," she says. "I think I've fallen under 'The Mayan Spell.'"

Chapter 33

MORE MEN

JUST ONE WEEK HAS PASSED SINCE TWO-THIRDS OF THE TRES AMIGAS have left and my next house guests arrive. It is also the week of the trade show—finally!

My one and only client (so far), whom I call The Funny Little Texan, and his wife have come to Playa, but I have their condo rented out, so they are staying in my second bedroom and have the run of the house.

A friend of The Funny Little Texan is visiting Playa this week, too. He comes over to my place to greet his friends. Funny thing is, it seems he's spending more time talking to me than to his friends. Hmmm… There's just one tiny little problem—his name is Mark!

❧ ❧ ❧

The family who I rented out my client's condo to seems to be very nice, at first glance. The father has survived a long battle with a life-threatening illness and has brought his family to Playa to celebrate life. He seems overjoyed and grateful to be alive. He takes in every smell, word, experience—savoring every breath of life.

"Oh, this condo is beautiful. The views are stunning!" he exclaims, when I first show him and his family the condo upon their arrival a few days earlier. He seems to be revitalized by Playa, much like me. I think I am going to like this man very much, until he comes to my condo one morning—alone.

141

The father says he needs to talk to me about something. His eyes are dark and distant, his gaze downcast, voice lower and slower. I'm thinking, *this can't be good.* I invite him to sit in the living room.

"You see, I sleepwalk," he starts. "I woke up in the middle of the night last night and went outside onto the balcony, probably to feel the fresh ocean breeze. I must have run right into the glass-top table on the balcony, because when I woke up this morning, the glass was broken into pieces and I had cuts all over my legs."

Then he shows me his cuts and they look pretty bad.

"Do you need medical attention?"

After he assures me he doesn't, my second concern: Is he posturing to blame me, my client, or the condo for his injuries? It turns out he mostly just wanted to report it to me and apologize. He says he will definitely pay to replace the glass in the table.

Then, changing the subject, he also asks me to hire a private chef to cater a traditional Mexican dinner at the condo and invites me, my client and his wife (who own the condo he is staying in), and my client's friend, Mark. He tells me he has also befriended a local shopkeeper on Fifth Avenue and wants to invite his family to join the dinner party, as well. *For a man who's setting up a party, he sure is talking in a somber voice. There is definitely something off about him today.*

He continues making small talk about Playa and his vacation and lingers a bit too long in my condo, like he's lonely and wants someone to talk to. There's a vibe I'm getting from him that's not quite sitting right with me, but I can't put my finger on it. I'm kind of feeling sorry for him, given his near-death experience and all, but then he leans in a little closer (you know, like in my personal bubble space) and says in a husky voice, "You are so lucky to live in Playa. I'll bet you have a *really* good time down here." And then he touches my hand.

Okay, creepy! This conversation is over. I stand up and tell him that I've got a lot of work to do, so I've got to get going. After he leaves, I notice that I'm kind of drained from that interaction. *Wonder what that's all about?*

℃ ℃ ℃

More Men

A few weeks prior I got a phone call from a friend of a friend I will call San Fran, because San Francisco is where he is living and working. San Fran was supposed to have gone to Cancun with us but ended up unable to make it (remember the "missing person?"). He called to talk about Playa, because he's thinking of moving and starting a business here and is coming to check it out in a few weeks' time. He heard through our mutual friend that I had just moved to Playa to start a business myself. I gave him the low-down on what making that move is actually like. We agreed to continue the conversation over drinks and dinner the first night he is in Mexico.

%% %% %%

He arrives in Playa with some friends exactly the same day as The Funny Little Texan and his wife arrive. I told you February was wild! Between hosting my client, his wife, their friend Mark and the renters in my client's condo, I am late meeting San Fran and his friends for drinks, but I tuck right in and begin to enjoy the party. First thing San Fran does is order a round of tequila shots for everyone. *Oh, I see how this night is going to go.* I'm not a fan of tequila shots, due to an unfortunate encounter with them a little earlier in my life. I tell San Fran this and ask for a margarita instead. But he insists. And this goes on all night.

I'm not really attracted to him, but he has an amazing energy and is great fun. Actually, it's the most fun I've had in a *long* time. He's a big flirt and oddly, when he flirts with the waitress, I find myself getting a little jealous. I know, completely crazy. What's even crazier is that I tell him so; "I know we're not on a date or anything, but I don't like you flirting with the waitress!"

He gives me a devilish smile and pulls me out onto the dance floor. At the end of the night, he offers to walk me home. When I oblige him by showing him my condo, my house-guests are thankfully awake, reading in the living room. After a quick tour of my place, I rush San Fran out the door before he gets any ideas. Besides, I've got a million things to do tomorrow to get ready for the trade show and this *chica* (girl) needs her beauty sleep.

Chapter 34

MAÑANA, MAÑANA

THE NEXT DAY, ONLY TWO DAYS BEFORE THE REAL ESTATE TRADE show, I run into my attorney. You may recall he advises conducting business below the radar, so I have a few covert elements to my operation. He says he's glad he ran into me because he wanted to warn me there may be government officials patrolling the trade show. *Oh, no!*

"What if they ask me for business documentation?" I ask my attorney.

"Don't worry. If they do, I'll bail you out of trouble."

This is so *not* reassuring to me. For the next two days leading up to the trade show, I am panicked. *Oh my God. This is not good! What if the authorities bust me? I don't wanna go to jail in Mexico! Do I go through with it? I've already spent three-thousand dollars for the booth and money for banners, brochures, etc. Shit.*

Ultimately, I decide I've already invested too much money and there is too much at stake not to go through with it. However, I notice that I'm beginning to feel increasing physical discomfort. *Maybe this is what an anxiety attack feels like?* Oh, well, I have too much to do to think about it. I have to concentrate on polishing my speech, getting banners made, flower arrangements ordered and all logistics finalized. The underlying tension and worry is greater than I've ever experienced in any undertaking in the States. I talk to myself: *Okay, I am taking risks and stretching myself, but is the trade show a good risk or a foolish one? It could either land me numerous new clients or land me in jail!*

❧ ❧ ❧

Tonight is the night of the catered dinner my rental client asked me to arrange. My Right-Hand Latina has a friend who caters, so we hired her to prepare the buffet of *pasole* soup, quesadillas, enchiladas, taco bar, all the trimmings and dessert. It is a festive evening and everyone has a marvelous time. Apparently, etiquette in Mexico dictates that you reciprocate a dinner invitation with a dinner invitation.

Consequently, the Fifth Avenue shopkeeper invites all of us to his house for a homemade, traditional, Mexican meal. I am so curious to visit a local neighborhood and I am so enchanted by the idea of dining with one of the locals at their house that I cannot refuse the invitation. Mark #3 quickly chimes in and suggests that he would like to escort me to the dinner. *I guess that means it's a date?*

After me, The Funny Little Texan and his wife return to my condo, I remark that I feel completely drained, kind of like my life energy has been sucked out of me. To my surprise, my client's wife says she feels the same way. She said this also happened a few nights ago when they and the couple renting their condo went out for drinks together.

❧ ❧ ❧

As I start getting my sales collateral together (brochures, handouts, and slide show), I ask my Right-Hand Latina, because of her marketing background, to step up and take over the marketing and sales materials. Because of her less-than-enthusiastic "yes", I am beginning to guess she doesn't want the responsibility or to make decisions on her own. Hmmm… perhaps women are not given the latitude to make decisions on their own in business in this country.

I am also realizing that everything takes four times longer than in the U.S. Even I, one of the most efficient people I know and who knows what needs to be done, am taking four times longer doing the tasks! *Why? Does the Mayan Spell have a bad side—a mesmerizing, hypnotic influence? I hope not.* Sure, Mexico is not caught up technologically, but the "*mañana, mañana*" attitude is insidious, seeping into the psyches of residents and expats alike.

I am grappling with a dichotomy: One philosophy says "do it now and get it done!" The other says "enjoy life now, work is not as important as living in the present." I discover pretty quickly the Mexican hierarchy of priorities, at least in this part of Mexico, is: 1) family 2) religion 3) pleasure and 4) work. (Sometimes numbers 3 and 4 are switched.)

When I try to embrace the second philosophy, I do notice I have less negative self-talk, less beating up on self, more enjoyment of the present. But with that philosophy also comes a certain degree of irresponsibility and resultant mistakes.

For example, I send my copy for all the sales materials to a print shop. I go to pick them up the day before the trade show and they don't look right. The graphics are not altogether good, and there are some misspelled words.

I tell them, "You guys gotta do these over and you gotta get them done for me today because I have the trade show starting in the morning."

And they're kind of like, "Yeah, okay, we'll do our best." The underlying attitude is, "Not really our fault lady that you've waited to the end." Which may be true, but in the U.S. the comparable print shop worker would say, "I'm so sorry, let me see how we can remedy that right now—our apologies." Don't they know customer service rule number one—the customer is always right?

℀ ℀ ℀

The next day, while I'm setting up the booth before the trade show starts, my Right-Hand Latina goes to the print shop to pick up the materials. But in true *mañana, mañana* fashion, the materials are not ready and she has to wait two hours, so is late to the trade show. The good news is, she also brings with her two gigantic, gorgeous floral arrangements that she's cleverly obtained for only fifty dollars. Our booth is stylish and inviting and we begin receiving visitors right away. My Right-Hand Latina does a wonderful job manning the booth and greeting people who come by. I realize how nice it is to have this collaboration and have high expectations for us as a team.

Chapter 35

TRADE SHOW REVELATIONS

A T THE TRADE SHOW, I MAKE A PRESENTATION AS A GUEST SPEAKER. I speak about having a condo in Playa del Carmen and point out all the ins and outs of vacation rental property ownership. This is great fun and I'm glad I've forced myself into doing this. Note to self: *It's not so bad being out of my comfort zone and I kind of like public speaking. Who knew?* After my presentation, I enjoy chatting with the parade of people who have approached me after my speech.

Perhaps, one of the most colorful people I meet is someone I now call, "Mexican Barbie." Although Caucasian, she manages an exotic impression that is part Latina *Telenovela* star with darkly tanned skin, part Marilyn Monroe with bleached-blonde hair and sexy body, and part Barbie Doll. We chat easily and I suggest we go to lunch at the trade show.

At lunch I find out that, like me, she has just moved to Playa. She says she's just landed a job selling real estate, which seems to be what most expats do in Playa to earn a living—probably because the Mexican real estate industry is not regulated and therefore you don't have to be licensed to sell properties. In fact, I know someone who met some tourists in Playa, took them to a few newly-constructed condominiums, and sold them one. He earned a ten-thousand dollar commission, and literally did nothing more than host these tourists for a few days. Crazy!

Mexican Barbie tells me she is also a musician and hopes to get her musical career going in Playa. She's already lined up a few gigs where she will perform in restaurants and nightclubs. I tell her I hope we can meet again, but before she says anything in agreement to that, she's flying off to her next activity, whatever that might be. Wow, how energetic she is, if a little flighty.

Right after lunch, in strolls San Fran. "Wow, what a surprise seeing you here," I say to him. "Where did you disappear to the last few days?"

"Well, you see, there's this woman I know who lives in another part of the Yucatán peninsula and we kind of made plans to see each other while I was here. I'm really sorry. We made these plans before I met you."

"Hey, don't be sorry. We didn't have any plans to hangout and I've been really busy with the trade show and my business and my client. No worries at all." *Hmmm… what a funny little exchange that was. Interesting that he feels obliged to me; yet in the daylight and stone-cold sober, I'm not the least bit attracted to him.* "Well, I better get back to my booth."

"Okay. Hey, you wanna go to the beach in Tulum tomorrow? I know this spot that is spectacularly beautiful and there's a little tiki bar on the beach that makes the best ceviche and margaritas."

"I never turn down an invite to the beach, and the best ceviche and margaritas. I'm in!" *Plus, since I'm not really interested in dating you, I don't have to feel self-conscious in my bikini.*

"Okay, I'll pick you up at your condo tomorrow at 11:00 a.m."

"Great! See you then."

’’’ ’’’ ’’’

About an hour later, the father of the family who is renting The Funny Little Texan's condo shows up at my booth and My Right-Hand Latina engages him in conversation while I'm chatting with some potential clients. After he leaves, she says to me, "Who was that man? My stomach is in knots after talking to him and I was really uncomfortable the whole time he was here. I feel like he was sucking the life energy from my body."

Yes, that's it! Now I can put my finger on it. He is a shape-shifting, life-sucking creature, just like in Star Trek (you know—the science fiction television series from the 1960s starring William Shatner)! Really clever how he presents himself as this grateful-to-be-alive, loving-every-moment-of-precious-life person; but in reality, he is sucking the life energy from everyone he comes into contact with. Seriously; there is something very alien and nefarious about this guy.

"Isn't it interesting," she says to me, "how the vibes people put out can so instantly create either a positive or negative effect on you?"

"I know," I said. "We must be alert and perceptive in sizing people up in order to avoid the ones with destructive intent."

❦ ❦ ❦

Not long after Life-Sucking Creepy Guy leaves, a chance meeting with a woman at the trade show adds to my awareness about being discerning of the people I invite into my life. This woman, of indeterminate age and description, is working at one of the nearby booths, or so it seems. I don't remember her name, but I'll never forget what she says to me, or her penetrating, grey eyes.

We are chatting and I'm telling her I have just moved down to Playa, am very excited about the move, starting this new property management business, and embarking on a new chapter of my life. I rhapsodize about how different I am in Playa; feeling light, happy and optimistic. She looks a bit skeptical like I'm looking at the world through rose-colored-glasses. Still, she listens carefully, nods and says, "I, too, moved to Playa—oh, it's been about three years ago, now." She pauses, assessing me as she asks, "May I give you some advice?"

I nod.

She clears her throat and narrows her eyes before saying; "I don't want to burst your bubble in the least, but I have to warn you that Playa has a very transient population. I want to advise you against getting involved with a man down here because from my very unhappy experience, I can tell you that most of the ex-pat men down here are usually running from something, either another person or the law."

I look at her, an intense woman with a steady gaze, but there is something else—an undercurrent of mystery. "Really!" I say. "That is very interesting and a bit scary, frankly."

She says. "I know, but please believe me when I say that you have to be very, very, careful getting into a relationship down here because everybody's running from something."

"Okay, I will."

She then tells me her horror story—that she'd fallen in love with a charming man who ended up being a criminal and ultimately conned her out of her life savings. She says that she had come down to Playa with the same attitude and joy I have, but also with a naiveté that she needed to outgrow. She sighs, "I had much to learn about the culture of ex-patriots."

I hear from more than one person that many expats are running from something they don't want to deal with back home. Could this include Batman? Mexican Barbie? And how many others I have yet to meet? *Am I running away from something?*

I tell her, "I'd really like to continue our conversation; but will you please excuse me? I have to attend to a visitor at my booth."

A few minutes later, I go to resume my conversation with the woman, but she's not in her booth. I ask another person sitting at her booth about when she'll be back and they look at me blankly—they don't know who I'm talking about. Hmmmm. It's like she's disappeared, for I don't see her for the remainder of the trade show. How very odd. She reminds me of those crones in mythic journey stories who appear, give a warning, and then disappear into the mist. In any case, I'm grateful she's woken me up and clued me in. Come to think of it, a few of the people I have met so far have a fairly significant character flaw. I ponder this a lot and want to understand this better.

❧ ❧ ❧

It turns out that the authorities do *not* come to check out my business credentials at the trade show. That's a relief and I am very happy I decided to do the show. By going outside of my comfort zone and investing a lot of time and money and mental energy in this trade show, I have expanded my network of possibilities and of people. Some of these people have been helpful, some not. I see that as my life is flooded with new people, I will have to discern who to trust and who not to trust.

Chapter 36

A Rosy Glow

SAN FRAN IS PERSISTENT! HE INVITES ME TO DINNER WHILE WE'RE at the beach in Tulum. He's seducing me with his upbeat, energetic and amazing personality and tales of the restaurants he owns back in San Francisco. On our way back from Tulum, a little tipsy from the margaritas, we sing to eighties rock bands such as Def Leppard, Van Halen, and Bon Jovi. I am having a really good time with this guy; really "letting my hair down" and letting loose.

%% %% %%

His last night in Playa, we have dinner plans with his friends at an upscale Argentinian Steakhouse in the heart of town. I am forty-five minutes late because I still have The Funny Little Texan and his wife at my condo, and their friend Mark is hanging around, too (a bit too much, for I have decided to ban "Marks" from my romantic life). When I do arrive at the restaurant, San Fran is relieved and annoyed at the same time. "We thought you were going to stand him up," announces San Fran's friend.

"I am so sorry," I say. "I still have my client at my house and we just got caught up in conversation. Besides, this is Mexico. Forty-five minutes late is akin to being early around here!"

"No worries," says San Fran. "Just drink up; you have some catching up to do!"

After dinner, I agree to walk to the beach with San Fran and he's really putting the moves on me. I am silently debating… *Do I or don't I? This is his last night in Playa. I'll probably never see him again. I've never had a one night stand in my life. Maybe I should try it, enjoy it and then say adios!* We go back to his hotel and canoodle by the pool for a while. If I didn't know better, I'd think he summoned about twenty hungry mosquitos to devour us. After I finally can't take getting bit any longer, I agree to go up to his room with him, which actually means it's a yes!

It feels really good to be held by a man again. I love it—it's been such a long time. After a few hours the good-girl voice in my head tells me that I need to get back to the condo, to my guests. Every bit the gentleman, San Fran escorts me safely home. And that's the end of the San Fran chapter of my life… or, so I thought.

℘ ℘ ℘

I am so grateful to My Right-Hand Latina for her help with the trade show that I am treating her to a spa day today. After our delicious spa treatments, we do a little shopping in the gift shop at the resort. As I'm trying on smaller-than-usual sizes, I realize that I've lost about ten pounds. I love the way I look, but don't love the way I feel. I feel off physically, somehow, but make the assumption that this will pass.

Afterwards, when we are leaving the resort, guess who I get a call from? Yup, San Fran. We have an animated conversation and after I get off the phone My Right-Hand Latina says, "You really like him, don't you? You are glowing!"

"It's true," I tell her, "I can't get him out of my mind!" I ponder this, *Maybe he's the reason that I'm in Playa. I just have this sense that I am here to meet my mate.* So much for one night stands—that experiment failed and I'm glad!

San Fran is gone and My Right-Hand Latina takes a week's vacation, so I get busy sending follow-up proposals to potential clients I met at the trade show. I also decide to go to Texas the following weekend to celebrate my Dad's seventieth birthday and to see my family. Emotionally and spiritually I am overflowing with affection for friends and family. I love being there for all the people in my life. Even though there are stresses with starting a new business, Playa has filled me up so much that I have much to give to others. In the magic and expansiveness of the last hectic weeks, I see that I've been attracting all these new people into my life and at the same time remaining in contact with old friends and family. Business-wise things are starting to gel and I feel I am really getting established in my newly created life. I am stimulated by my new man and intrigued by my new friends.

%% %% %%

High on my list of new friends is Mexican Barbie. She invites me to come watch her play guitar and sing at a local bar one night. I hope she's good so I don't have to feign praise and admiration.

I'm slightly late and squeeze into a little table in the corner, trying not to be noticed. And then between songs she says over the microphone, "Hey, there's my friend Brooke."

I give her a little wave, hoping that people will stop looking at me. She starts singing her next song, *in fluent Spanish*. I almost gasp. Her voice is extraordinary; it transports me to a higher wavelength. I am floored at how good she is. During her break, she comes over and says, "Hey, thanks for coming."

"Wow, you are amazing! You have the voice of an angel."

"Thanks. Singing is my passion."

"I can tell. So how did you get this gig?"

"I simply walked in here earlier today and said, 'I sing and play guitar,' and they hired me on the spot."

"C'mon, who does that?"

"That's how I usually do it around here."

After the gig, we go for a walk down Fifth Avenue and I can't help but notice that every man is gawking, practically salivating over her. What's more, she is greeting every one of them by name. She must know every man in Playa between the ages of thirty and fifty! Normally, I would

WHY YOU NO SCREAM VIVA?!

be miffed that my friend was getting all the attention; but for whatever reason, I am perfectly happy to be getting the ancillary benefits of being Barbie's sidekick. *And who can blame them for gawking at her; she is drop-dead gorgeous!*

In every way, she has the potential to be a star and, with the addition of a good agent/coach, I am certain that she will skyrocket to greatness.

158

Chapter 37

My Two New Best Friends

Speaking of star potential, about a week after the trade show ended and my guests departed, I'm walking down the road in front of my condo building when I happen to see an adorable Labrador walking his owner. But the poor pooch is limping pretty badly.

As we approach each other, he looks at me and says, *Hey lady, got any treats in that handbag?*

No, sorry; but what happened to you? The closer he gets, I notice he looks too skinny and I think, *you sure look like you could use some treats.*

When we reach each other, I say to the dog walker, "What happened to your dog?"

"He's just had surgery on his hip. Several nights ago, we saw him wandering down Fifth Avenue, looking for scraps of food and limping around on three legs, so I brought him home with me. I took him to the vet the next day and they did surgery to repair his dislocated hip. He's a real cutie, eh?" she says in the tell-tale Canadian vernacular.

He was at least twenty pounds underweight. You could see his spine and the narrow of his back was only about two inches across.

"Yes, he is adorable. I love dogs and miss mine terribly."

"What kind of dogs do you have?"

"I have two golden retrievers, River and Meko. My ex is keeping them back in the United States while I'm down here in Playa starting a property management business. Are you going to keep this sweet pooch?"

"Well, I live in this building," she points to my building, "And since we are just renting, I am not allowed to keep him."

"Hey, I live in this building, too." We then introduce ourselves and I continue, "So, what are you going to do with him?"

"Do you mind if we continue our conversation inside, where Dexter can rest comfortably? He's been on his feet for a while and I'm worried about his hip giving out."

"Not at all. Dexter, huh? How'd you come up with that name?"

Inside her condo, she continues, "I named him Dexter the Dog—it just sort of suits him. We have a friend who owns a restaurant in Playa who said he'd take him in. He has a home on the outskirts of Playa with a big yard and he's got two other dogs, so he'll have some companions, too. After a few weeks of rehab at my house, I'll take him to his new home."

We talk for another hour and a half and I can tell we'll be good friends—she's open and easy to talk to and we share a love of dogs. We talk more about dogs and then move on to people. And so our relationship unfolds.

Dexter's Mom, as I will call her, turns out to be the most solid, trustworthy person I know in Playa—the exception to the warning the Crone gave me that most people in town are running from something. She and her husband are expats making their home base here in Mexico.

℆ ℆ ℆

Over the next few weeks, I bond with Dexter. He religiously gives me wet, sloppy kisses and nuzzles me between my knees to acknowledge my arrival. He becomes my surrogate furry companion, in the absence of River and Meko.

During our daily walks to rehab Dexter, I've come to realize that Dexter's Mom is an unflinching observer of human nature. We spend countless hours analyzing the people that we have met here. While I tend to give people the benefit of the doubt and ignore the negatives until it's too late, she's a bit more judicious. She studies people in great detail so that she has the ability to predict their behavior, and therefore escape future complications with them. She inspires me to see more deeply into character. About Athlete, for example, she says in her forthright way, "Athlete is extremely intelligent, but there is something 'a bit question-able' about him." She turns out to be right.

And regarding Mexican Barbie, although Dexter's Mom sees how talented and well-meaning she is, she warns me against getting into the money-making schemes in Playa that Barbie seems drawn to. We discuss how many people fall prey to get-rich-quick schemes, usually run by criminals, and how devastating the consequences can be. Although we admire Barbie for doing whatever it takes to be self-sufficient and to create the life she wants in Playa, we conclude that she takes imprudent risks. *I am really fond of Mexican Barbie, but I wish she would just focus on her talent and gifts and not get distracted so easily.*

I talk to Dexter's Mom about other people in my life who have aspects of personality that are uncomfortable to me. She and I discuss the mirror philosophy—that people come into our lives to mirror us so that what we don't like in others, we can correct in ourselves. "You know, the mirror philosophy works," she says, "but sometimes people are just being jerks and you have to deal with it."

I laugh and admit "Yeah, I probably need to work more on recog-nizing the jerks and steering clear of them. I am more than willing to self-inspect when I don't like what I see in another person, but I do want to understand why I attract the people I do into my life."

Dexter's Mom continues with her philosophy of being wide-eyed and alert. "Well, for example, there is somebody in our building who I suspect is dabbling in drugs, or illegal gambling or something. I'm not going to mention any names; but you probably know him."

"How do you know?"

"Well, I don't *know* for sure. All I know is there have been some shady-looking folks coming and going in that condo and the *Federales* raided his condo one night and it was disturbing, to say the least."

"Holy shit! When did that happen? Did they arrest him?"

"I don't know, but I don't think so. Open your eyes, Brooke. Corruption and shadiness is all around us. You just have to be willing to see it."

૭ ૭ ૭

Later we hear that the neighbor she was referring to was running a gambling operation where he'd invited some big money people to the game, invitation only. Apparently, this was a little too close to the drug cartels' turf and they "persuaded" him to shut it down by tipping off the *Federales*. And then the neighbor left to go back to the states for a while. Hmmmm…

After spending time with Dexter's Mom, I conclude that I should further develop my powers of observation. Perhaps this will help me to avoid disappointment with this transient cast of characters. And perhaps I will discover when to be dismissive and when to be tolerant of their flaws. I find that I'm grateful to Dexter's Mom for her integrity, and for helping me to confront the complexities of human nature, while still embracing people with a spirit of celebration. I aspire to this.

Over a short period of time, our friendship grows and we discover that our greatest bond is still our shared love for dogs, especially Dexter! Little did we know how bonded we were about to become over this dog.

Chapter 38

Dexter, Have You No Shame?

COME EARLY MARCH, I HAVE TURNED DOWN TWO NEW CLIENTS (too small and too far away) and lost two bids to manage the units of an entire building. I'm two months into this new property management venture and I still only have one client. Maybe I need some distance to evaluate things. February was such an intense time of change, after all. I think about a nice distraction and my first thought is of San Fran.

So, I e-mail San Fran and ask, "What do you think about a little rendezvous weekend after next? I could probably sneak off to San Fran for a weekend." He calls me immediately and says, "What date and what time? I'll be at the airport to pick you up!" *Hmmm, I guess men like it when women take the initiative.*

❧ ❧ ❧

I go for four dreamy days, full of adventure and new experiences. How refreshing! The first night we go to dinner at one of his favorite restaurants. He introduces me to the owner, and to his friends—making me feel special, pretty, and desirable all at once—I'm floating on cloud nine! He even surprises me and takes me to his home in Lake Tahoe for the weekend. This visit with San Fran fills up both of us.

Upon my return to Playa, I see Dexter at his Mom's condo. I stop by to say hello and inquire as to the occasion for the doggy's visit. His Mom tells me she checked on him at his new home and he was doing terribly—miserable from being left outdoors with indifferent care, so she immediately took him back. In fact, he is still twenty pounds under his ideal weight. *Unbelievable! Who could neglect this sweet little guy like that?*

So Dexter's Mom and I talk it over and agree that, since we are willing and able to take care of him, we should keep him. I will be the official caretaker, since I am allowed to have pets; but he will mostly live in her condo, except when she travels to Canada and then he will live with me. We further commit that whether we are living in Playa or elsewhere, we will both make sure to take care of him for the rest of his life.

Nourishing him with ground burger and tuna fish in his kibble, Dexter's Mom and I, in just two weeks, help him gain twenty pounds. That makes me even madder at his previous caretaker. Poor Dexter was still starving, even under the care of a human being! *Geez, people, pull your heads out!*

We've both heard that swimming is the best way to rehab a hip, for humans and canines alike, so we decide to take him for a dip in the ocean. We are warned that dogs are not allowed on the beach and could be confiscated, so we go early before the tourists hit the beaches. The first time we take him to the ocean, he is terrified, which is surprising because Labs usually love the water. We quickly surmise that he's never been in water. We have to show him how to go in the water and swim, and once he figures it out, he loves it. We watch him turn into a puppy in the water because he's so thrilled.

One morning while exercising Dexter, a woman approaches us on the beach and says "Hey, is that a 'fox red pointing lab?'"

Dexter's Mom and I just look at each other with a dumbfounded look on our faces, shrug our shoulders, and reply "I dunno."

The woman says, "I know it is; my parents used to breed them." The woman looks at Dexter and says, "*Sienta te.*" And promptly Dexter sits down. "*Ir a buscar,*" she exclaims as she throws the ball into the water and off Dexter goes to fetch it.

Unbelievable! Dexter's Mom and I look at each other, our jaws dropped. He is a full-blooded, bi-lingual Fox Red Pointing Lab. Who knew we had such a celebrity on our hands? I'm sure his previous owner must be devastated.

But she leaves us with a harsh warning. "You better be very, very careful about sneaking your dog onto the beach and into the water. The police do patrol, and if they catch you, they will take your dog from you, and they are not nice to them when they're in doggy jail." She scares us so badly we just stop taking Dexter to the beach. A real loss, but it isn't worth the risk to us. We will find ways to give him lots of exercise—more walks, for example. I was about to find out what a celebrity he really is on one of those many walks.

As a full-blooded retriever, Dexter always has to carry something in his mouth. One night, we're walking down Fifth Avenue, and he is nudging me, driving me crazy to carry something. Finally I figure out that he wants to carry my handbag. It is this cute little bag that I got in Playa made of coconut skin with wooden handles. So I hand the bag over to Dexter and he dutifully takes the handbag in his mouth and starts prancing down Fifth Avenue with his head held high. He becomes an instant star. (See, I told you I could spot talent a mile away.) People point and laugh. Tourists stop us and ask if they can take a picture of this tall, red labrador retriever carrying a ladies' handbag down the main drag. I, of course, oblige. *Who am I to deny sharing this endearing moment?*

At first I am afraid his jaws might get tired and he'll drop my handbag in a mud puddle or on the street where someone could grab it and run. Wrong! He has jaws of steel. Dexter is better than having an armed guard to protect my handbag. He carries my bag for many, many blocks and when I get to my destination, he's not about to let go of his precious cargo. Now who looks like a spectacle? It looks like *I'm* stealing the handbag away from my dog! Needless to say, we've got to work on the obedience command, "Drop it."

Chapter 39

THE MORMON WAKE-UP CALL

MARCH IS A BUSY TRAVEL MONTH FOR ME. FORTUNATELY, I AM still doing contract work for the company back in Denver, which keeps my coffers filled while I'm establishing my new business (which is taking longer than I had thought). About two weeks after returning from my weekend rendezvous in San Francisco, I head back to Denver for an in-person assignment. While there, San Fran asks me to come visit him again on my way back to Playa. And once again, San Fran and I have a great time. *Could he be the one?*

I'm disappointed to find out, upon my return to Playa, that My Right-Hand Latina did not answer any rental inquiries while I was away. She seems to be losing interest, though not in her paycheck. About this time, Athlete stops by my condo one night with a bottle of wine he wants to share. This seems very odd because he never just "comes by." While we're chatting and drinking wine, I tell him I'm considering getting out of property management altogether. The work is not rewarding, and there is too little benefit. That's when he tells me he has a business proposition for me. *Okay, something's got to change, so I'm listening.*

"So, you know that I work abroad and travel frequently," he starts. "And while I'm away, I'd like to rent out my condo. I'd like you to do some minimal property management for me."

"What exactly do you mean by minimal?"

"Well, I'll do all the advertising and the initial contact and contracts with the clients. You would greet them upon their arrival and be their go-to person in case they need anything while they are here."

He says it will be a kind of co-management arrangement. *It seems easy enough.* I agree to do this on a trial basis. It is income, after all, and I do need to consider alternative business models at this point.

Not long after this conversation, I get my first project from Athlete. I meet and greet his clients at his condo at the appointed time. They are a very nice family of Mormons from Utah—a dad, mom and three girls. I get them all checked in, tell them about the local sites to see and places to eat and see that they are well situated. This was a pleasant enough experience and I love to be needed this way—as a meeter and greeter!

Later that night, I attend Dexter's Mom's fiftieth birthday party at one of the nicer restaurants in Playa. We eat, drink an abundance of wine and really have a jolly time. I get home about midnight and all I want to do is to undress and fall into bed. Just as I'm putting on my pajamas, however, there's a knock on the door.

It is the dad of the Mormon family. When I open the door, I see that he is frowning and quite unhappy. I'm embarrassed to be in my PJs, but I know it must be serious if the tenant knocks on the door after midnight, his face pinched with extreme distress.

I'm mortified. Did I mention that he is Mormon? Last I heard, Mormons abstain from the use of alcohol and here I am, quite tipsy, unpresentable, and unprofessional. But like a firefighter responding to a fire alarm, I will have to sober up quickly, and become a professional ready for an emergency.

"Sorry to bother you, but we cannot go to bed because the sheets on the beds have not been washed," he says.

My words come out like a kind of thoughtless stutter: "Oh… my… God…, I am so sorry. Oh, shoot. I shouldn't have used the word God like that. Sorry again. I will take care of this. Could you give me just a minute to get dressed?" *And to figure out what I'm going to do?*

He nods solemnly. I partially close the door and get dressed in about thirty seconds, telling my mind and body to sober up *now*. But I have a dilemma. I don't know Athlete's condo at all! I don't know where he keeps his clean sheets, assuming he has clean sheets. I was just supposed to greet the clients. So the only thing I can think to do is take all of my clean linens down to make sure that they have clean linens for their stay. I gather up all my linens and follow him to Athlete's condo and make up the beds while the sleepy family watches me. I feel like I'm on stage, but the "wine high" has definitely worn off, chased away by a kind of fury and disgust for Athlete.

After making up the beds, I go back up to my condo, and phone Athlete and read him the riot act, the gist of which is: "What the hell were you thinking?" and proceed to tell him the whole story.

"That's bullshit," he says. "I washed those sheets and bleached them three times before I put them on the beds."

"How naïve do you think I am? I saw the dirty sheets myself."

"Well, they were clean. That's all I know."

"Well, that's the end of our business arrangement. That's all *I* know."

Despite that hiccup, the Mormon family does have a nice time and I learn a good lesson: Partial responsibility is risky; with full responsibility, I can ensure things go right. I conclude that I do not want to do property management for anybody unless I have complete control over the condominium, so I'm glad I told Athlete I'd pulled the plug on our co-management arrangement. From now on, any unit I manage will be cleaned to my standards and I will know where everything is and how to handle anything that comes up.

When I discuss my disappointment about Athlete with Dexter's Mom, she gives me a sidelong look. "Didn't I mention there was something 'questionable' about him?"

"Yes, but I wanted to give him… I mean how do you know when to give someone the benefit of the doubt and when to steer away?"

"You develop a kind of instinct or intuition, based on observation. And then you have to learn to trust it."

℗ ℗ ℗

Next thing I know, my Right-Hand Latina proposes a new business arrangement to me. She wants to get into a linen rental business, renting linens to my property management clients. I really don't see how it will be cost effective for me or my clients (especially since I still only have one client), but with reluctance, I agree, wanting to help her establish her own business and feeling a little guilty that mine has not taken off yet as I had hoped. I suppose I had a tiny bit of hope that this new service would enhance our business, but as I suspect, it does not turn out to be a good financial decision for my business. *What are my instincts telling me now?*

Chapter 40

DESTINY TO THE RESCUE

DEXTER'S MOM INVITES ME TO A DINNER PARTY THAT SHE AND HER husband are hosting at their condo to celebrate Mother's Day. As it turns out, she was a caterer in her life "BP" (Before Playa) and she loves to host intimate get-togethers at their condo, preparing a yummy home-cooked meal for everyone. This is the second one I've been invited to; the first was an Easter feast in March, where she made a roast turkey with stuffing, baked ham, rice potatoes with gravy, green bean casserole, jellied salad, corn, buns and butter. For dessert we had what is affectionately referred to as "finky" dessert—chocolate wafers layered with whipping cream. For Mother's Day, she is making a similar meal and asked me to bring some wine to share. I feel like she and her husband are my adopted family since we are starting to celebrate holidays together. It's interesting to learn about Canadian holidays and culture, too. Some holidays are the same as U.S. holidays (like Easter and Christmas) and some are not (like Thanksgiving). However it seems as though we celebrate with very similar feasts!

%% %% %%

Not long after Mother's Day, My Good Neighbor (remember the one who invited me to enjoy his air-conditioning one evening last year when I failed to pay my electricity bill?) calls and says he is coming to visit Playa and could he stay in my guest room for a week because his condo

171

is rented out for the season? Well, one good deed deserves another in my book, so I say yes.

While My Good Neighbor is staying at my place, Mexican Barbie decides we should have a party on my beautiful rooftop terrace and volunteers to organize an all-night jam session under the stars (the first of many) with her talented, eclectic musician buddies. The characters who show up are lively and gifted. It is comical watching them traipse up my very narrow spiral staircase with their large cases filled with musical instruments. The music floats through the beautiful spring air, and lasts all night. This is where I learn to love Flamenco music with its sizzling, fast-paced rhythm. Music lifts me up to a kind of joy and optimism, nothing else can do in this particular way.

During his visit, after seeing how happy I am and discussing the merits of living in paradise, or perhaps being enchanted by my new friend, Mexican Barbie, My Good Neighbor decides he wants to move back to Playa and asks if he can continue to stay with me until he can get his own place. My intuition tells me to say no, but I agree—with more than a little reluctance.

All is going fairly well with my new temporary roommate, until about two weeks later when I gain another roommate—making us three. Mexican Barbie is planning to go back to Canada for a while and needs a place to stay for a week, as her lease has expired and she has to move out of her apartment. At some point during this time, it seems as though My Good Neighbor reveals his amorous intentions towards Mexican Barbie (which he denies) and something happens that makes her furious. This kicks up quite a firestorm. There's way too much drama in my household and I am not enjoying it one bit. I am disgusted and disappointed not to have my safe, happy haven. *What is with all these disappointments?* If only I'd listen to my intuition.

As if he's tuned into my ups and downs in mood, and much to my delight, San Fran invites me to attend a wedding with him during an upcoming visit stateside, and I am all too happy to accept. I miss the rejuvenation and love I feel with San Fran. Anyway, My Right-Hand Latina is off for a two-week vacation with her husband, so I don't have to worry about keeping her busy. I leave and ask My Good Neighbor to find another place to live—and please, by the time I return.

While I am visiting San Fran, one night he says, "I've got an idea. You may think this is crazy; but why don't you come in July and spend a month with me on a trial basis to see if we're a long-term match?" *Gulp. Hope rises up in me as if attached to an eternal spring. Maybe this so-called distraction is really a major part of my future dream, my destiny?*

Chapter 41

WHAT AM I MISSING?

Well, let's face it, I'm contemplating throwing in the towel on my business in Playa—it's not fun or even profitable at the moment. Why not get away for a longer time, get some perspective and also see if this intriguing man is the guy I've been searching for?

🌀 🌀 🌀

On the night that I arrive in San Francisco, the earth suddenly stands still as San Fran surprises me by saying, "I think you are the one, Brooke."

Wait! These are the right words, but is he the right person? I am elated, yet, at the same time my gut tightens into a painful knot. Why? Is it that I'm just not sure yet? Isn't that what this next month is about—to find out if we are each other's destiny? Besides he's had a bit to drink and so can I trust him under those circumstances?

My instincts tell me that something's not quite right, and despite what Dexter's Mom keeps drilling into me, I fight that knowledge, wondering if there might be something wrong with me. Why am I not happy to hear those words from him? Those are the very words that I've been wishing to hear.

And then it happens... I implode. Every mishap and mental malady connected with a long line of "wrong" guys hits my mind like a bomb and I have a meltdown of histrionic proportions. It's as if every romantic dream that has ended—crushed on the rocks of misalignment and misunderstanding—hits me like a tsunami of sadness; it washes over me in wave after icy wave that I cannot stop.

It shocks us both. San Fran does not know what to do or say and just stares at me like I'm a stranger he never expected to meet. The experiment is clearly going to be a disaster. We both go to bed but do not make love.

The next day, both of us are still somewhat in shock and denial. As emotional as I was the night before, today I am just that analytical and reasoning. And so is San Fran. We are both trying our best to be adults about our situation, so, we go ahead with our plans to go to Tahoe. Unbelievably we are together there for some weeks, trying to salvage what we had. We only partially succeed through a lot of denial and politeness. Not surprisingly, San Fran does a one-hundred eighty degree turn about my being "the one." Eventually, we both acknowledge in voices of reason, that we are not going to fulfill the roles that each of us needs and wants. *Big sigh…*

I can't wait to get back to the comfort of Playa. I need my special space. And, it is a place, I still believe, that I can sort out the problems of my life that ironically have grown in size since being in Playa. I need something more than romance or distraction now. I need to take the bull by the horns and stare down these problems. But I'm going to need some kind of help I haven't yet enlisted.

PART SIX

Getting Grounded and Moving On – Listening To Spiritual Messages

∽ ∽ ∽

We are not human beings having a spiritual experience;
we are spiritual beings having a human experience.

~ Pierre Teilhard de Chardin ~

Chapter 42

LISTENING TO THE PHYSICAL BODY

WHILE IT IS TRUE THAT PLAYA HAS BEEN MY DREAM PLACE, THAT it comforts me, embraces me and I heal here, something is wrong now. My body has been trying to tell me something, using a slew of symptoms, but I haven't been listening to or deciphering the messages.

The first sign that something is not right starts with sore and swollen joints so severe that I'm having trouble walking because my feet hurt so badly. I am unable to turn the doorknob of the front door without great pain because my hands ache something awful. I think, *Is it the humidity? Except that doesn't make sense since I grew up in Texas where there's lots of humidity and I didn't have joint problems there.*

At about the same time, I lose my appetite again. I recall how I lost all of that weight after Marc #1 and I broke up. Looking back, I realize that I felt unwell as I prepared for the trade show. By the time I was dating San Fran, I'd lost more than ten pounds. The next body issue happens around March or April with sores on my skin that are excruciatingly painful. Out of all the things in my life that have been stressful, including the break-up with Marc #1, never has there been anything that has caused me such physical pain. Haven't I been healing here in this peaceful place? This series of maladies is shaking me to my core. I don't know what to think about all of this… I only know that it hurts.

When I go to see one of the doctors in Playa, who is Cuban, he's unclear about the diagnosis of what's causing the sores on my skin, but sends me to the drug store to get a prescription, which I take immediately. Shortly thereafter, I notice that the whites of my eyes and my skin start to turn yellow. It's the freakiest thing I have ever seen in my life. I run to the internet and look up my symptoms. My research brings me to the obvious conclusion—*I'm dying!*

Before reassessing my will and making plans for my final days, I decide to confirm my diagnosis by revisiting the doctor.

I ask, "Am I supposed to be turning yellow?"

Nervously he says, "I want you to go to the emergency clinic right now! I think you may be having kidney failure and I need x-rays of your kidneys." I waste no time getting to the ER. The interesting thing about the emergency clinic here is that, while it's pretty old-fashioned, it's actually fairly efficient. You have to pay cash for x-rays or MRIs or whatever you're going to get, and they give you the x-rays right there on the spot to take back to the doctor. I'm in and out in an hour, I don't have any billing issues to deal with, no insurance to deal with, and I walk out with my x-rays. And the news is good—my kidneys are fine.

The Cuban doctor now starts hypothesizing; it could be cancer, could be this, could be that, all terrible things. I'm like, *Holy shit! I want to go home! I want to go home to a doctor that I trust.* I don't have any confidence in him, and yet he's supposed to be the best in town, but here I am, turning yellow.

Finally, my common sense kicks in and I decide to stop taking the medicine. Sure enough, within a couple of days, the yellow disappears and I am back to *looking* normal by all outward appearances, but I still have blisters on my backside that hurt like hell.

When I return to the States to see my primary care physician in Colorado, the sores are scabbing and healing. Since she can't swab and test them to know for sure, she could only look at them. She is certain, however, when she says, "Okay, you have 'shingles.'" *Well, that sounds rather disgusting!* But at least I have an answer that dispels my worst fears. She informs me that it's the chicken pox virus brought to 'life' by extreme stress and suggests that I take a good look at the sources of stress in my life.

※ ※ ※

I've been running so fast and furiously since I moved to Playa that I haven't been able to take stock, as my U.S. doctor suggested, until now. I am finally stopping the merry-go-round to look at any and all possible sources of stress: things in my environment, things in my psyche—anything that could be causing all these illnesses and conditions that I've never had before. I list my considerations: *Maybe I've been overwhelmed by the overload of living in a new country and, more or less leaving everything that's familiar behind. Maybe in being on my own, starting a new business, I've been stretching out of my comfort zone, most of the time. Maybe it's all the disappointments—in love, in business, in myself?*

All of these, I'm sure, have contributed to my physical symptoms. But how could that be? I love that I am stronger and bolder, living the life of my dreams and doing exciting things…Yet, I am stressed out and my body is rebelling. What an interesting paradox.

My favorite place to ponder such things is the beach outside my condo. So I wander down there, put my feet in the waves and think about how to have an exciting, adventurous, fulfilling life without all the associated stress.

The Mayan Spirit once again demands that I breathe in her beauty and healing forces. I do. The deep breathing and meditation begin to heal me and I remind myself to practice yoga regularly. But there is a persistent question that does not go away: "Is living and working in Playa right for me right now?"

Chapter 43

LISTENING TO
THE INNER VOICE

A<small>S I EXAMINE THE QUESTION, TO LEAVE OR NOT TO LEAVE PLAYA,</small> I realize again that visiting paradise and living in paradise are two totally different experiences. When you're visiting paradise, you get this bird's-eye view, swooping in, doing fun things, being romanced by the ambiance, the people, the experiences, and then going back home to your modern conveniences in a modern world.

When you're living and working in a newly industrialized world, (aka Mexico) you realize day in and day out, that there are many inconveniences and barriers to efficiency—not the least of which is the language barrier. Then there's the endless dust (from living where there are dirt roads), the humidity, the bugs, and the skin rashes that contribute to low morale. And then there's the "*mañana, mañana*" attitude that contributes to the lethargy. It's not the same idyllic picture living in paradise as it is visiting paradise. However, you would never know that until you come and live here. So this whole self-discovery adventure includes the observation of how I've unwittingly compromised my standards.

When you are visiting paradise, there's not much compromising of standards demanded because you are in an alternate universe of sorts. And if one does compromise, it is temporary. One of the fun things about vacation is you get to be a totally different person if you want to! You can be wild and crazy or just a pleasure seeker twenty-four seven, and you only have seven days to do it, let's say, so you fit in a lot of touristy things that inspire and revive you. It is called "vacation" for a reason; you vacate your life in order to have rest and recreation.

But I've not been on *vacation;* I've been pursuing *vocation.* Because I'm working so hard, I have not been enjoying the pleasures of Playa like I'd done before starting a business here. One day my neighbor from Italy, with shoulder-length, wavy, sandy brown hair and the most beautiful crystal-blue eyes I've ever seen, comes by my drive-through window and says in his thick Italian accent, "Bella, why are you working again? You're *always* working. You must go to the beach! It's a beautiful, sunny day. Why are you in *here,* Bella?"

While I want to say, "What the hell, let me grab my towel and I'll go with you," what I really say, while playing the martyr a bit, is, "Well, you see, Bello, I have to work if I want to get this business off the ground. I'm the only one who cares enough to do it."

I feel a self-pity party coming on. I sigh, feeling so serious and conscientious. I sense that if the business fails, it won't be a big deal for My Right-Hand Latina; she has less invested in it. She's all for the upside, but she doesn't want any of the downside. So that's part of it. I have this wobbly business to run mostly by myself and there's this self-enforced pressure to work, to make a go of it. So, back to my question: "Is living and working in Playa right for me right now?" I really need to talk this over with someone I trust and I know just who to call! I need some advice from my trusty pal, Kim.

"*Hola,* Kim! *Que pasa*?" I say when she answers.

"*Hola, Amiga*! How's my favorite *gringa* pal?"

"I'm doing okay, but I need someone to bounce some things off of. You got time to talk?"

"Sure. Whatcha got?"

"Well, I've been debating whether or not I should stay in Playa and try to make my business work or move back to Colorado and go back to work in the corporate world, where I can make a lot more money with a lot less effort. As I look at my property management business, I have to be honest with myself and admit that in seven months, it's not really going anywhere, and maybe even more importantly I am not really enjoying the work and the struggle. There are so many things that make it difficult to succeed in business down here, but more than that is how much I've had to compromise personally with my standards in work and relationships. I also feel this pull back to Colorado, which I can't really explain."

"You need to trust that feeling," Kim interrupts my monologue.

"I've weighed all the pros and cons of living in both places and they come out about even. But for some reason, it seems as if Colorado is calling me. If I'm really honest with myself, I want to be in Colorado more than Playa right now."

She says, "Well, then, that's your answer."

"Yeah, you're probably right." I take in a deep breath and let out a big sigh. "Thanks, Pal! You're always such a great help."

"All's I did was answer the phone!"

"And listened to me, silly. Anyway, I always feel more confident in my decisions when I have your blessing."

"I'm happy to give it. And, Pal, trust your good instincts, okay?"

༄ ༄ ༄

With Kim's nod of agreement, I start preparations to move back to Colorado. Mexican Barbie has been staying with me ever since I returned from the month-long experiment with San Fran. She was housesitting Dexter at my condo while both Dexter's Mom and I were away from Playa during July. I tell her she can stay in my condo after I leave Playa, until I get it rented out; but in exchange I need her to help me, by overseeing some maintenance I need done on my condo and my client's condo. Mexican Barbie, who has the best intentions in the world, says she knows of a handyman from her church, named Steve, who she'd like me to hire to do the maintenance work.

Condominiums in Playa require an enormous amount of mainte-nance. The sea and salt air is really harsh—on the wood, the paint, the hinges, and the water taps. That's one of the reasons, in hindsight, I shouldn't have been so impulsive about buying a place in Playa.

Steve has a hard luck story—he's a recovering alcoholic who was not paid on his last job for a lot of work he did. Consequently, he was not able to pay his workers either. So, Mexican Barbie is trying to help him out by finding work for him. And since he seems well qualified to do the work, it makes me happy to help him out as well.

Steve gives me a bid for all the projects, on both mine and my client's condo. I've been told by the church he goes to that he's been attending Alcoholics Anonymous, is married with many children and goes regularly to church. So, I hire him.

It is standard practice in Mexico to give workers half of the money up front because they need the cash to purchase materials for the job. So I give Steve half the money up front and tell Mexican Barbie to give him the second half when the work is *done*, as I will be residing back in the States when the time comes.

I also contact Dexter's Mom and ask her if she is interested in taking over my property management business. She has told me several times before that she really wants to find some work or to do something productive with her time. She is interested and we agree to discuss it when she is back in Playa. I let my Right-Hand Latina know that I am shutting down the property management business, thank her for her service and wish her well in all her other endeavors. As my plans to turn over some of the things I need to do in Playa seem to be falling into place, I book my flight back to Colorado for a month from now. But then, something peculiar happens to me as I'm spending one of my last few precious Sundays hanging out at Mamitas Beach.

With my toes in the water and breathing deep of the sunset and sea breeze, I receive an urgent message, intuitively. I feel a magnetic pull—something is beckoning me back home again to Colorado, not in a month, but *now*. I don't know who or what it is, but it seems so pressing and strong, that I resolve to follow it. I am on the next plane to Denver.

Chapter 44

LISTENING TO AN UNSEEN VOICE

A T THE TIME I RETURN TO COLORADO, IT BECOMES CLEAR WHO IS beckoning me. My first day back, Marc #1 tells me that River, our twelve-year-old golden retriever, has been diagnosed with advanced cancer. I figure it out—she must have been getting sick about the time I moved to Mexico. *Damn.* The first thing we have to do is have her enlarged spleen removed—a major surgery. As a result of the surgery, her coat goes white, she stops eating and does out-of-character things, like refusing treats and not coming back inside the house. *Oh, my heart is aching. She's aging so rapidly in front of my eyes.* Over the next few weeks, she continues to deteriorate and there's not a damn thing I can do about it. Throughout this time, River persists in her message to me: *Something's not right—I'm trying to tell you something else is wrong.*

Suddenly, the cancer worsens and goes to her spinal cord and blinds her. When she goes blind, Marc #1 calls me from the veterinarian clinic in the middle of the night. I rush over to the clinic. Together, we decide to call Cindy, our animal communicator friend and ask her to commune with River, to give us what she's feeling and saying.

Cindy is agreeable and tells us River is grateful for the time with us and that she's getting ready to leave us. After we hang up from Cindy, I ask to be alone with River. I feel completely confident I can do this on my own now. I get centered.

Talk to me, River. I say telepathically. *Tell me anything else you want to about how you feel and what you need.*

Suddenly a wave of grief, her grief, washes over me and I really hear her.

When you went away, I felt you had left me forever. I missed you. I love Dad (Marc #1); but I couldn't live without my mom. You are irreplaceable.

I gasp back my tears. *Oh, my little girl, did you get sick so I'd come back?*

I don't get an answer to that, but her tail wags a little and an immense feeling of love fills the room. *I never intended to leave you forever. I love you, girl, I will always love you. You are such a good dog—you have been such a blessing to me.*

More tail wagging and she lifts her head and looks up at me, face to face.

I continue, *Do you know how much I love you?*

Yes, she tells me. *Yes, we share a great love.*

Oh, River, thank you. Thank you for that great love.

Chapter 45

LISTENING TO THE AUTHENTIC VOICE

WITH THE LOVE OF MY SWEET DOG LINGERING AND BEFORE I CAN recover from her loss, Mexican Barbie sends me an e-mail that signals that the wheels on my plan in Playa are starting to fall off. She writes that all the teak furniture inside and out was finished, but she's afraid it's not what I asked for. All I had wanted Steve to do was to sand it down and put a clear sealant on the furniture to bring out the natural color of the teak wood and protect it. Instead, they stained all of my beautiful teak furniture a dark brown. I call her up.

"Dark brown? Damn it, it's probably ruined," I explode into anger.

Mexican Barbie starts to backpedal by saying, "It looks beautiful; I think it looks beautiful!"

I say, "Not what we discussed and it's not what I asked them to do. Not what I want! If I wanted dark brown furniture, I'd have bought dark brown furniture. I bought natural teak furniture." I try to calm myself, but I'm too incensed. "Barbie, I wanted the natural teak color maintained. It's very, very expensive furniture. I want it looking the way it looked when I bought it."

I don't like the sound of my voice, it's harsh with anger and accusation, but I can't help myself. I am so frustrated with people's incompetence and their taking advantage of me.

"I mean you have to see it, they did a careful job…"

189

"Barbie, I left you in charge of this project in exchange for free rent in my condo and I expect you to do the project as I've instructed. I don't care what you have to do; I want my teak furniture restored to the color it was when I bought it."

I must have shaken her. I don't remember who hung up first, but her voice was tentative when she said goodbye.

A week later, Mexican Barbie calls and says she needs the rest of the money for Steve. I tell her again that I've already given Steve the upfront money, so to be sure all the work is done before giving him the rest of the money. I'm very clear about this. And then I wire her the money.

A few days later Mexican Barbie calls me again. "I'm afraid I've got bad news."

"Bad news? *(as if the earlier news was good?)* What now?"

"Steve told me he didn't get enough money upfront, so I took him down to the money place and gave him the remaining money you wired to me."

"Damn it, Barbie, what part of 'don't give him the rest of the money until the job is completed' did you not understand?" My voice goes high with rage.

"Wait, it gets worse."

"Really."

"Yeah, Steve disappeared, nobody can find him, I've tried, the church has tried…"

"Give me his number. I'm calling him right now."

"Don't bother; his phone's been turned off."

"Oh my God. Well, what are you going to do about it, Barbie?"

Barbie goes on to explain that she had contacted the pastor first thing, and when the pastor couldn't reach Steve, he told Barbie that he and some of the congregation members would finish up the jobs, and in fact have already started the work. She goes on to say that nobody ever heard from or about Steve again and they think he went back to binge drinking.

What a mess. *Oh Barbie.*

After I hang up the phone I notice that expressing my anger so openly is a weight off my shoulders. I am not used to expressing anger like that. I never expressed anger in my relationship with Marc #1. It actually feels good to stand up for myself. Now I can move forward.

I end up paying my client back for the work that didn't get completed out of my own money because I think that is the fair thing to do. I'm mad at myself that I've delegated this to Mexican Barbie and she's botched it. I do give her credit for being brave enough to call me and tell me the bad news. And I have to own the fact that I didn't choose someone I knew was more competent to oversee this kind of project. This lesson costs me about eight hundred dollars.

It isn't a lot of money, but it's the final straw for me. I'd done everything I knew to do as a businesswoman. I had him give me an estimate, I had it in writing, I signed it, he signed it. My eyes were opened once again and it was time for me to make some changes that would help me detect flakes and unreliable people.

As if that little episode wasn't enough to send me over the edge, another disturbing thing occurs after I return to Colorado. My Right-Hand Latina writes me a nasty email saying I owe her, per Mexican law, three months of severance pay. *What? Are you freakin' kidding me?* I am livid—shocked at her gall. I've never heard of that law; but even so, she certainly does not deserve severance pay.

She has taken six weeks of vacation (much of it paid) over the last five months, she has not stepped up when I have been traveling, and she has been asked to do very little work over the past few months. Yet, I have paid her dutifully, without question. I've treated her to a spa day, I've brought her presents from the states. I've supported her linen business to the financial detriment of my own business. In fact, of the two of us, she's the only one who's gotten paid in this business so far. I feel I have been overly generous with her and now she says I *owe* her more? Plus, my Mexican lawyer tells me the law doesn't apply in this case.

I am so upset by this situation that I haven't been sleeping or eating well at all. I think I am most upset that she is challenging my integrity and fairness with her. We exchange some sad and strained emails and finally I agree to pay her one thousand dollars in the hopes of putting an end to this drama, gaining some peace of mind and saving the friendship. She agrees and that ends that, but the friendship never recovers its original camaraderie and enthusiasm. I am left wondering why a few of my once-cherished relationships are disintegrating before my eyes.

In retrospect, my anger with both women seemed justified. I was expressing negativity, but my expression didn't change the outcome. However, it changed something in me. I now feel that expressing anger can be the most healing and authentic thing to do. When people communicate with each other from some place other than their authentic selves, the communication is ineffective, at best, and toxic, at worst. It is really clear to me at this point that when I responded to Mexican Barbie I was being authentic and when I responded to My Right-Hand Latina, I wasn't. I should have stood up for myself better, even if it meant losing a friend.

Wow, does the learning ever stop? I guess not, since we're all works-in-progress. But, how can I be authentic with people and maintain the good feelings between us? I really want to know.

Chapter 46

LISTENING TO THE MAYAN VOICE

WHAT I DO KNOW IS THAT I HAVE TO GO BACK TO PLAYA. I TELL myself I need to go back to tie up some loose ends, inspect my furniture and the repairs in my client's condo and to finalize business arrangements with Dexter's Mom. But deep down, I know that I have to go back to resolve the lingering bitterness I feel about the betrayals and the lack of competence that showed up in people I really liked and believed in. When I arrive, I have to handle some things the first day, but still feel upset the next day when I awake to see my now "beautiful" dark brown furniture. Mexican Barbie has moved out and is not around. Just as well, I suppose. It would probably just exacerbate my anger and sore feelings.

I decide to walk down to Mamitas Beach, where I have often gone over the last eight months to ponder my life. I watch some swimmers float and bob on the ocean swells. Inside, my anger is still eating at me so I try drinking up the healing air of Playa to calm myself.

In the past when I have felt lost or upset, I learned that gaining control over a situation makes me calmer because I *feel* like I'm in control of my life. Consequently, I have tried hard to be in control of *everything* in my life, but that's not working right now—not at all. I give up! Somebody or something, give me an answer here!

As if on cue, a biplane with a banner floating behind it flies overhead. I squint my eyes to see what the word is on the banner but the sun is in my eyes. However, I think it reads *forgive!* Oh, my God, a series of chills zip down my spine. I got my answer.

Forgive. Forgive yourself and forgive others.

Tears form in my eyes and I try to stop them which makes my throat hurt—but this kind of tears is confirmation that what I'm getting is the truth. I do have to forgive. I have to forgive Steve. I have to forgive Mexican Barbie. I have to forgive My Right-Hand Latina. Hell, I even have to forgive Marc #1.

I have to allow people to be human, allow them to have flaws, as I most certainly have them. With that thought, something that only later I realize is my old friend, the Mayan Spirit, sends a surge of warmth to me—lifts me up—and my body relaxes like it hasn't for a long time. I am beginning to realize at least a big part of my spiritual liberation comes from letting go of negative feelings and obsessive control; surrendering "to what is." Later I will fully learn that forgiveness is essential to surrendering and surrendering is essential to spiritual freedom.

I realize that in expecting too much and then becoming disappointed, I bring hurt upon myself and disharmony with others. I'm listening now. To what? I like to think it is the voice of some ancient Mayan Spirit. I absolutely feel that something is leading me. After all, apparently I need something big to wake me up! In any case the message comes: *Brooke, don't expect too much of people but rather see what gifts they bring into this world and accept and admire those.* Hmmm… The "Law of Acceptance:" Today I will accept people as they are; not how I want them to be.

Now, I can just hear Dexter's Mom's voice in my head, "Mirror philosophy, remember the mirror philosophy."

I remember how Dexter's Mom and I discussed this. When a person irritates you, see what it is in that person that might be mirroring something negative in yourself. I will have to contemplate what it is, if anything, that Mexican Barbie is reflecting to me. I am not incompetent, that's not it, but maybe I don't honor my own creative talent enough—she tends to not let herself be as successful artistically as she obviously should be. I mean, her talent is extraordinary! Or maybe she relies on her beauty too much. Do I rely on my looks for too much of my power?

I can also hear Dexter's Mom's voice saying, "Don't forget to be constantly wide-eyed and on the alert, too! People can be devious." I have to laugh; she's so down-to-earth and I need that grounding right now (even if it is only a voice in my head).

I feel the urge to go back to the condo and call Mexican Barbie, for forgiveness has softened me, given me a renewed appreciation for our friendship. After all, we did create some of my favorite memories of living in Playa and I'd like to celebrate my Playa friends with one last jam session/party on my roof. On the way back to my condo, the biplane is flying back the other direction. I glance up at the banner to get confirmation of my revelation and see that the banner reads "Free Drinks at Coco Bongo!" *That must be another biplane. I know what I saw!*

I feel excited about planning this get-together but when I try to call Mexican Barbie, I can't reach her. The same is true with some of my other friends, I can't reach them, either. *How strange. Maybe this is a sign from the Universe that I'm not supposed to be with people right now. Yep, I have a feeling the Mayan Spirit is not through with me yet! Okay, maybe there's another lesson to learn.*

I vow to pay particular attention to my dreams tonight, looking for a sign and they do not fail me. I have a strange dream about being a Mayan high priestess or something like that; but then suddenly I am being sacrificed in an important ceremony. I am pushed off a high cliff, but then I could fly. At the moment of soaring, I woke up. *What the hell does that portend?*

Today, I feel drawn to get on a bus to Tulum. *How strange.* I don't know quite where I'm being led; but by the time we arrive, I know I have to find my way to the beach below the ruins at Tulum. I feel chills all over my body, a strange combination of fear and exhilaration all at the same time—mystical, magical. It seems like I'm not really controlling this journey now; I'm really aware of being directed.

As I walk, I think about how I'd been lured to this particular part of the Mayan Riviera to make a home—an area where so many seekers before me lived thousands of years ago, pondering the mysteries of nature and the universe, just like me. The parallels do not escape me.

I mull over how the sacred grounds give off a powerful energy. If it hadn't been for my dear friend Kim, I would have never experienced that special energy that blew us away at Chichén Itzá. I send up a thank you to Kim and for a second, wish she were here. Alas, the Mayan Spirit probably wouldn't allow her here anyway, as this is apparently a time for me to fly solo.

So, I just keep walking and pondering. The ancient Mayan culture has been saying our world is due for a shift of unfathomable magnitude. I feel drawn to the mysticism of the Mayans. Thinking about that gives me chills again. Yes, I am a down-to-earth, action-oriented woman, involved in the shifting sands of career, romance, and friendship. But I have to admit I'm becoming a believer in intuitive paths to truth, not the least of which is telepathy. And now this strange feeling like I'm being guided and spoken to. More chills and warm flows, alternately.

After walking and walking, I've lost track of time, and the mundane, little things of everyday life fade from my consciousness—my concerns of late seem so small and insignificant. I ask the sacred grounds, *What is it you want me to know? Is there something more you want me to know about myself or my fellow human beings? Give me a sign, please.* I stop and look around. I am half expecting to see a fish jump out of the water or bird swoop in and poop on my head. But I get nothing. I continue to walk, deciding that I will keep walking until I do get an answer. With each footstep I notice my shadow is getting longer and longer and the light is increasingly ethereal as Sunset is approaching. Now I'm a little worried. Am I having a Mexican standoff with the Universe? Who do you think is gonna win this one?

For hours I have walked, no one in sight—only jungle, sky, sands and an array of flowering gifts—this place, this earth, this universe is indeed abundant. I no longer think, I am beyond thought, so I just look and I am filled with gratitude. My journey finally brings me to the edge of the water. *Oh, this blessed sea!*

Standing in the waves, intuition after intuition laps at my consciousness and I feel more filled with a kind of knowing than I've ever felt before. I gaze at the waves crashing upon the shore, then pull back into themselves. I watch this rhythm over and over until I am in some kind of meditative trance. I feel like I'm open to hearing something important, but again, not with my human ears.

The overriding message, expressed in a poetic voice comes to me on the next set of waves: *Daughter of the Earth, bring your sisters back to us, let them find their own wisdom here, let them hear with their own ears the messages they need to hear. Tell your stories so they can courageously discover their own.*

Wow… I don't have to give up Playa? I just need to share her?

The voice pervades my body.

Yes, share what you've learned here.

"But I've failed here, in so many ways—my business, romance, some of my friendships…" My voice hitches as I cry this out loud, a lump in my throat as big as a rock.

There is no such thing as failure, ultimately, there are just lessons that you either learn from or not. You've learned a lot!

"I have? What?"

Look in your heart. You know.

I do this. But, I keep hearing the voice as if it is outside of me and yet reverberating through me. It's weird, but interesting.

The Mayan Spirit is more emphatic. *You have learned within these ancient lands and energies to charge at life boldly, to open your arms to life, fearlessly.*

"Yes, I have, haven't I?" I say aloud, amazed at myself!

You have also learned when to pull back and see what you have done, look at the consequences of your choices, nurture the good ones and, as needed, make better ones going forward.

"Yes, like the waves, I crash forward, then draw back. That's life, isn't it?"

By now the Mayan Spirit and my voice have blended just as the waves from different directions meet at the shore. I see I can be happy alone because I have my own voice more fully now! I am both listening to myself and to the wisdom available to me spiritually. How much more there must be than what I've tapped into in all those years when I was so careful to control everything.

I am not just happy in this moment but ecstatic! Exhilaration moves me and I start to run along the beach, my feet splashing in the incoming waves. I feel like I can fly; I'm lighter than air. The Mayan Spirit has set me free!

℆ ℆ ℆

And then I hear her; I hear barking, coming from the waves, way ahead of me, out in the sea about thirty feet. I squint to see better. It's River, swimming towards shore, through the surf, then splashing down the edge of the surf towards me. She's leaping like she did as a puppy. I'm so happy to see her so exuberant, healthy and so *herself*. Tears of joy fill my eyes, spill and wet my cheeks. I reach out my arms to her.

When my tears clear, she's gone. Oddly, I am not sad. I feel strengthened, strong. I wrap my arms around myself and feel their warmth, her warmth. I'm happy she's come to me, even in a vision of setting sunlight and reflection. She's told me she's whole, she's herself again. *Wow, just like me!*

River's happy nature is in me, will always be in me. *Oh my God*, I realize, *love never leaves us, love for family, for friends, for beloved pets, for everyone I've ever loved… it does not erase, ever. It is always there, part of our ever-growing, ever-learning souls.*

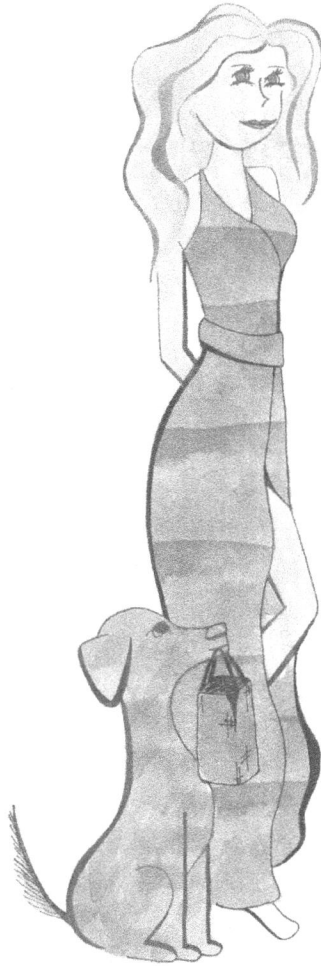

Don't ask yourself what the world needs;
ask yourself what makes you come alive.
And then go and do that. Because what the
world needs is people who have come alive.

~ Harold Whitman ~

EPILOGUE

THANK YOU FOR COMING ALONG WITH ME ON MY ODYSSEY, *WHY You No Scream Viva?!* Not only on this string of adventures, but really, in every stage in our lives we learn over and over that out of adversity and negativity come growth. Perhaps you agree that rarely do we grow and call forth our true fortitude and valor when everything is going perfectly well in our lives. In fact, I'd venture to guess that a lot of people are "sleepwalking" through their lives until some major adversity strikes. That was true for me.

And now you have seen that since I wasn't paying attention, I was led to take a little journey. And that journey allowed me to find my spirit (me) again. I had allowed part of my essence to get snuffed-out in my relationship and even more so in the aftermath of the broken relationship, when I wrongly concluded there was something terribly wrong with me that made me unlovable and undesirable. Yes, I did and do continually have to admit to my flaws, my fragility as well as my strengths. But the journey under the Mayan Spell revived my spirit, so that I could soar again, and at the same time coaxed me into being a realist so that I could changes things from how they are, not from how I wish things could be.

The journey depicted in this book was about overcoming heartbreak and let-downs and finding the silver lining in everything that happens. That is quite a skill—to find the good side to even the most painful events. I am still working on developing and practicing that skill.

In becoming a single woman again, I had the privilege and freedom to make choices. I got to choose what I wanted and what I didn't want: how I spent my time, what I did with my body, who I trusted, who got to be my friend, whether or not to always follow the law, taking on responsibility for another living creature. I learned that it's okay to experiment with choices. In retrospect, I see that the best choices I made on this journey were first of all, the choice to not be a victim and second of all, the choice to create happiness and gratitude every day, no matter what.

I learned that what really makes my spirit soar is being grounded and adventurous at the same time. I didn't feel comfortable with the transient nature of people in Playa del Carmen. At the time, I felt that people seemed to be running from something and so was I. But I was also being drawn towards independence, spontaneity, self-determinism, entrepreneurialism, and a daring/courageous life. And while I chose not to create a permanent life there, Playa opened my eyes to new adventures, new opportunities, new people, and new cultures. Playa gave me wings, but it did not ground me, and I needed both.

We are all works-in-progress. I learned in Playa that most people are composites of many attributes—good qualities and not-so-good qualities—strengths and weaknesses. Most of us are full of contradictions. And while most of the friends I made in Playa disappointed me on some level, they all gave me extraordinary gifts that were critical to my healing, growing and seeing life and people in a more realistic, inclusive and grounded way. One of those friends taught me about having fun and spontaneity. One of those friends taught me about selflessly lending a helping hand to people. Several of those friends taught me to create a "personal policy" around responsibility and delegation to other people. On balance, I'd say my life was enhanced from crossing paths with these people. In fact, I now know that all people I cross paths with will enhance my life in some way, if I allow them to—including (and perhaps especially) my romantic liaisons.

I had a dream, it got tarnished, then revamped. My dream of living in paradise didn't look like I thought it would. Initially, I was looking through rose-colored glasses and not at what is. However, Playa did bring me the new life I really sought, it just happened to be in Colorado. I am so grateful for my home there, my family and friends, my modern conveniences, my solid grasp of the English language, and the structure and stability that comes from living in a developed country. I took all these things for granted, until I experienced them from another perspective.

I still have my place in Playa—a beautiful, inspiring space that I want to share with others, especially women as they face their next steps in life, their second chances or their desire for greater enhancement. Playa feeds the soul like no other place and my workshops offer nurturing and inspiration to those who take them. Moving to Playa del Carmen was the most empowering decision of my whole life (so far) and I wouldn't trade any of it for anything. It was an adventure like none other and I treasure every painful and exhilarating epiphany. I can own, now, my part in the imperfection of relationships, of any failed endeavors, the hurts I received and also bestowed on others. I also embrace my new-found compassion, strength, courage and ongoing sense of humor and fairness.

My deep felt thanks goes to all the people who shared in my adventures. And my thanks to you who came along to share in my stories. I hope you are empowered to make better, livelier, more honest and more spiritually fulfilling choices for you.

My parting words: Get out there! Go ahead and dream. Take some chances. And always remember to find the silver linings. Scream *viva*, my dear readers, scream *viva*!

Acknowledgments

WRITING THIS BOOK WAS A JOURNEY UNTO ITSELF. SOMETIMES I wrote in free-flowing joyous states and sometimes I avoided writing like it was the plague. What I realized is that this book had a life of its own and this baby was not going to be birthed before its time. Ah, the journey continues… Consequently, I had a lot of encouragement and sometimes some gentle prodding (Susan) to get me over the finish line.

First and foremost I want to thank my dear friend Kim Magee. She truly is a heroine and epitomizes selflessness. I aspire to be the kind of friend that she is. She was such a huge part of this journey (and still is). Little did she know what a ride she was getting on! And she was a big help filling in some of the blanks on some of the stories, where I'm pretty sure I had blocked them from my memory. ☺

I also want to thank my creative team: Susan Stroh, ghostwriter; Patricia Ross, publisher; Kaitlyn Whyte, artist; and Ronda Taylor, book designer. Susan is a kindred spirit for sure. Her expert and professional guidance helped me bring my stories to life. Her kind and loving spirit helped me articulate my message beautifully. And her gentle, but persistent, push helped me get this book finished so I could start the next chapter of my life. Patricia's encouragement, mentorship and guidance through the publishing process was invaluable. The artwork that graces the interior of my book was drawn by the lovely and talented Kaitlyn Whyte. She captured the images I wanted to portray exquisitely. Ronda, who designed my book cover and the interior, is super talented (obviously) and is also a kindred spirit in that she walks the same path to self-empowerment as I do—literally!

WHY YOU NO SCREAM VIVA?!

I'd especially like to thank the Marks: Marc #1 and Mark #2. Some of the learnings from you were the hardest—and greatest. But, I will likely never forget them. As they say, no mirror is as accurate as those in a romantic relationship. You stretched my ability to love and nurture myself and for that, I will always be grateful. And thank you to all the other past and current romantic partners for being my teachers and helping me to grow. My life has been enriched by each and every one of you.

I'd also like to thank all the colorful characters in my book, who are real people; but whose names I have changed to spare them any unwanted notoriety: Dexter's Mom, Mexican Barbie, Right-Hand Latina, San Fran, Athlete, Batman, My Good Neighbor, The Funny Little Texan, Life-Sucking Creepy Guy, Quatro, Mi Maestro, GQ and all the other characters in my stories. You have all been gifts in my life and shown me that every life is meaningful and valuable, if not perfect, if only we take the time to see and appreciate the mirror standing in front of us.

I have several special friends I want to thank who support me in everything I do. I feel their strength and wisdom always. Thank you Cindy & Bruce Hartzell, Shelly Labac, Doni Luckett, Kem Anderson, Kim O'Connor, Leslie Hahn, Kim & Tom Whyte, Jeff & Rowena Randall, Denise & Patrick Juliana, John & Sandra Fischer and, of course, my mom and late dad.

There are many more who have encouraged me along the way. So thank you to all my family, friends and acquaintances that cheered me on and said they'd love to read my memoir.

My list would not be complete without giving a great big, wet sloppy thank you to my four-legged friends who make this journey on earth so much more delightful. Thank you River, Meko and last but not least, Dexter the Dog!

Join the Sisterhood

Tell your stories and hear with your own ears...
I would love to hear from you about the insights and lessons you may have gleaned from my stories or from similar stories of your own. I believe we learn from each other and I would be honored to hear your comments or reactions about my journey or to hear advice you've learned along the way on yours. Post your insights on my blog at www.screamviva.com and I will endeavor to respond to all of you!

You heard the Mayan Spirit. She would love to have you hear with your own ears the messages you need to hear. I facilitate ladies' retreats in Playa del Carmen right in the same condominium where these stories took place, so that you too can hear and feel the Mayan Spirit. Come create your own stories in this experiential workshop. Visit our website at www.vivaclubmexico.com or Facebook page Why You No Scream Viva for more details and upcoming dates.

About the Author

Brooke & Dexter

Brooke Martellaro lives nestled in the pines of Colorado with her golden retriever, Meko. She loves golfing, traveling, wining and dining with friends and discovering new adventures. After spending twenty-plus years honing her skills in the highly-structured corporate environment, Brooke set out on her own to use those skills in helping women and entrepreneurs succeed. Brooke founded and is actively involved in several dynamic organizations, including Viva Club Mexico, inspiring women to reclaim their joie de vivre through engaging workshops and adventure travel. At Viva Club Mexico, in the Riviera Maya, guests attend morning classes overlooking the Caribbean and then embark upon activities ranging from ecotours to dance lessons to volunteer work. They later enjoy R&R in the form of beach time and afternoon siestas, gathering afterwards on the balcony for cocktails and a debrief session. The day ends with a magical evening at one of the quaint local restaurants in Playa del Carmen. When not in Mexico, Brooke is helping entrepreneurs navigate the growth stage of their business though her company Springboard Ventures. To have your own "scream viva" experience or to learn more about Brooke, visit www.screamviva.com.

www.ingramcontent.com/pod-product-compliance
Lightning Source LLC
Chambersburg PA
CBHW072138090426
42739CB00013B/3221